D1402253

The University of Texas
Institute of Latin-American Studies

Latin-American Studies

X

TITLES IN
LATIN AMERICAN STUDIES

The University of Texas
Institute of Latin-American Studies
Latin-American Studies, X

The Anatomy of Eleven Towns
in Michoacán

BY

DAN STANISLAWSKI

GREENWOOD PRESS, PUBLISHERS
NEW YORK

Originally published in 1950
by The University of Texas Press

First Greenwood Reprinting, 1969

Library of Congress Catalogue Card Number 69-19010

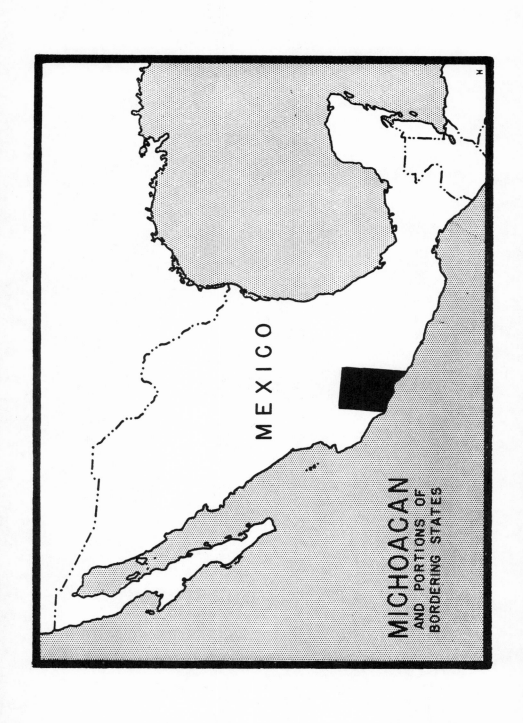

MEXICO

MICHOACAN
AND PORTIONS OF
BORDERING STATES

The Anatomy of Eleven Towns in Michoacán

The towns of Michoacán have distinct personalities. Of this I was sure after several field trips into the state. But "personality differences," although readily felt, are not easily expressed. A method was needed to determine these differences, one that would indicate them in a manner useful to geographers.

In the small towns of Latin America the home is also the center of most economic activities. The major exceptions to this are trading in the open market and farming. This being the case, it seemed probable that if a record were made of all dwellings and the economic activity of each, the information, when placed upon a map, would show distributional aspects that might indicate differences between towns. Through this the elusive quality of these differing towns might be understood.

To procure such information I had to canvass all dwellings or get the information from informants. In the latter case I used always two and sometimes three informants for the same area to be certain of accuracy.

For mapping, all activities were arranged in four major categories: (1) stores, (2) crafts, (3) administrative offices, and (4) services. In addition to this, a subjective estimate was made of the quality of each house.

I chose eleven towns to study. One is located in the coastal mountains of the southern part of the state; three are in the low Balsas valley; and two are in the contact zone between the hot Balsas valley and the temperate slopes to the north. Four are within the mountain valleys of the volcanic ranges, and one, the highest, is on the cool slope at about 8,000 feet elevation.

These towns were chosen originally because of an assumption that each would be strongly influenced by its geographical area. From this assumption it seemed probable that a town of one geographical area would exhibit intrinsic differences from a town of another area. From this it was inferred that the four towns in the mountain valleys would show similarities due to their environment, and that the Balsas valley towns would show similarities to each other but differ from those of the mountain valleys. These assumptions were quickly shattered by the analytic maps. It became obvious that the geographical region could not explain the differences between the towns except in part.

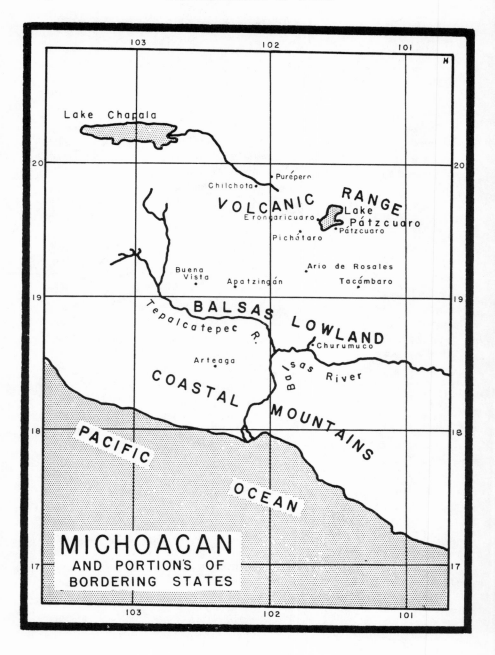

It has long been recognized, not only for Spain and the Spanish New World but for other parts of Europe and North America as well, that importance and prestige is associated with the central square, plaza, commons—whatever it is called. In Latin America this tendency seems to be accentuated.

In studying and comparing the maps made of these selected towns, the overwhelming importance of the plaza in some towns and its neglect in others was obvious. That this is directly correlated with racial and cultural backgrounds makes it fundamental to the interpretation of the results of this study.

The position relative to the plaza in Hispanic towns is also a rough index as to the value of property. This is also true, although less obviously, in relation to the main arterials. It is not possible to place exact money values on property, either for business or residence, but Hispanic informants never hesitated to express the opinion that the best property was that on or near the plaza or on the arterials.

Among the eleven towns studied, some are of basically Iberian character, others are of the New World with sixteenth century innovations but not in sufficient numbers or strength to nullify the essential Indian character. A third group must be noted. It cannot be accurately called mestizo or blended because it possesses both pure Indian and Hispanic qualities rather unmixed.

It seems logical to classify all of these towns in terms of two basic culture groups, Hispanic and Indian, with a third category, the dual-character town.

Under these major categories a further breakdown must be made in terms of function, but function altered by geographical position and time of settlement.

The Hispanic towns are: Pátzcuaro, Ário de Rosales, Tacámbaro, Purépero, Apatzingán, Buena Vista, Churumuco, and Arteaga. Erongarícuaro is a dual-character town, rather more Hispanic than Indian. Chilchota falls within the same category but is more Indian than Hispanic. Pichátaro is Indian with its character essentially unaltered by the fact that the stores of the town are largely mestizo owned.

The Coastal Mountains

The remoteness and relief of this region have maintained it as one of the least known of all Mexico. It is an area predominantly of crystalline and metamorphic rocks. Upon these are lying sediments, chiefly limestones and shales.[1] Stream cutting has made deep incisions exposing the oldest rocks. Promontories, separated by spectacular canyons cut by the short but swift stream, are typical features.

Few outsiders have traversed the region. One who has gives this description:

> The trail was a crumbling shelf, dug out from the face of precipices. I had not felt dizzy until today. Now, as the stones rolled from under the mule's skilled feet and dropped into abysses, I doubted my head. We crept along, the boys on foot and careful not to interfere with the animals nor give them any advice. Against my left hand was the mountain, under my right hand, nothing but such a valley as I had never seen, except once in Bolivia—so broad, so far below. The distance across it left the mountains on the other side in haze, and it began here so abruptly that to look straight out made one's senses swim. Let Briza catch a light hoof in a vine, and we would dive into space. Between the dark cliff that grazed my boot and that shimmering emptiness there was only Briza. I could not watch the cargo mules, picking their way. These, indeed were "serious mountains."[2]

There is little to attract men to these mountains. The soils are thin and the steepness of the slopes and canyon walls has precluded the use of all but a small part of them. There are no snug, fertile little valleys here of the kind that are found in the volcanic Mountain Region lying on the other side of the Balsas Lowland.

A description of the climate can be made only in the most general terms, for there are no weather stations and no statistics. Field experience plus the observations of permanent dwellers are the sources of information.

It is probable that the seasonal and total rainfall of the south slope is comparable to that of the corresponding slope of the Volcanic Mountain system. This would mean a yearly total of 35 to 50 inches, varying, of course, with exposure and elevation. It is concentrated in the summer months with only occasional light "unseasonal" rains as a consequence of abnormal cyclonic conditions in the Pacific.

At the lower elevations of the seaward slope the humidity is high through parts of the year. One is warned that all possessions of value should be wrapped carefully to protect them from rust or mould. At slightly higher elevations dense fog is relatively frequent.

---

[1] Vicente Gálvez, *Hidrogeología de la Zona de Aguililla*, 9.
[2] Marian Storm, *Hoofways into Hot Country*, 93.

As might be expected, the inner (northern) slope is much drier. The total rainfall and the average relative humidity are considerably less.

The moisture difference between these two slopes of the Coastal Mountains is reflected in the vegetation. The seaward slope exhibits a more thriving appearance, especially on the lower slopes. The dominant species roughly correspond with those of comparable elevations on the slopes north of the Balsas Lowland. They are mostly leguminous, a large proportion of the individuals being members of the Senna (Caesalpiniaceae) and Mimosa (Mimosaceae) families.

There is no road across these Coastal Mountains in Michoacán, and only one commonly used mule trail—that passing through Arteaga, where the mountains are lower and the slopes less precipitous. Even there the descent is not easy.

This is a little known part of Mexico. Few enter the region from outside and the permanent inhabitants live without moving far from the place of their birth.

With regard to its economic status this area makes a poor comparison with other major regions of Michoacán. Having almost a quarter of the total land of the state, it has but 1 per cent of the population, with a density of three persons per square kilometer. It has no town with a population exceeding 2,500 and is, therefore, listed as being entirely "rural" by the Mexican census (1940).

Economic activity is limited almost entirely to the planting of meagre crops in small subsistence plots and to pastoral pursuits. Only 4 per cent of the total land is in cultivation. The crops consist of maize, beans, tropical fruits—chiefly mangos, guavas, and plantains, a little tobacco, sugar and sesame, and a few coconuts.

The production of maize per hectare falls far behind that of all other regions. The production of beans is so poor that in many places they have to be imported. A small quantity of tobacco is exported, as well as small quantities of fruits. Plantains are raised on the coastal slope below Arteaga, where they are basic to the diet.

Pastoral pursuits are of slightly greater importance than agriculture. The Coastal Mountains lag far behind the other regions of the state in the number of cattle and hogs (the only important animals raised) which do represent, however, the greatest source of cash income for the region.

These pursuits, meagre as they are, occupy virtually all of the people. The percentage of persons engaged in industry, communication, and transport and commerce is small. There are a few unimportant *trapiches* for making brown sugar, and a few individuals devote a part of their time to making hammocks and pottery. The few mining properties are of no great importance.

Most of the population of the region lives in ranchos of a few huts each scattered throughout the hills. Only a few of the settlements can be termed "towns." A half dozen such count their

Rancho on the slope of the Coastal Mountains

inhabitants in the hundreds. Only three are important enough to be singled out. Each of these is seated at about 3,000 feet elevation. Two report a population of over 2,000 each, and one claims 1,300.

Arteaga

Two small streams have their beginning on the seaward slope of the Coastal Mountains of Michoacán at about 1,000 meters elevation. A few miles below their sources they converge in a small, relatively level valley. Level land and water being at a premium in the region, the site of present Arteaga has obvious advantage.

It is probable that the site was used long before the Conquest. But, if so, it was merely one of many ranchos or small villages of too little importance to be given place on the record.

It seems likely that growth to approximately its present size took place in the nineteenth century, at which time it entered into the official record.[3] Two reasons may account for its growth. Gold may be the first. It has been produced since the nineteenth century by primitive methods from several little mines on the

Milling gold ore. Coastal Mountains below Arteaga

slopes nearby. The second reason was, it seems, political. Just before the middle of the nineteenth century the chaotic conditions of Mexico and especially in parts of the states of Guerrero and Michoacán led to the migration of people, the abandonment of homes, and the search for refuge in remote areas. Some of the present inhabitants of Arteaga tell of the flight of the families

---

[3]José Guadalupe Romero, *Noticias para formar la história y la estadística del Obispado de Michoacán, México*, map facing p. 32. Also, *Memoria presentada por el ciudadano General de división Manuel González al ejecutivo de la unión*, 83.

from Guerrero and other parts of Michoacán to get beyond the area of revolutionary activities. Some of the families who moved into the area at that time had been engaged in trade elsewhere. This may have been the reason for their choice of this site. For in addition to water and relatively level land, Arteaga lies athwart the route from the mouth of the Balsas to the best pass in the Coastal Mountains. The town is just one "jornada," one day's mule trip, from the coast, and it has ample pasturage.

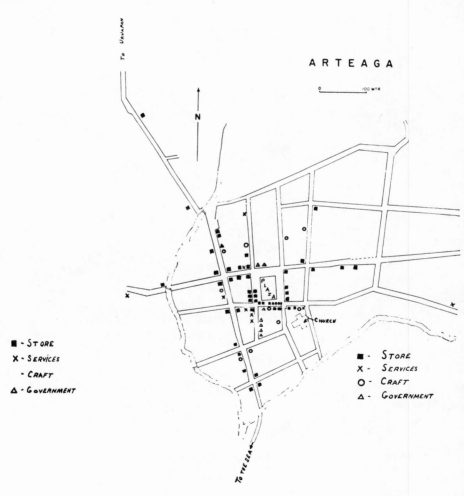

ARTEAGA

■ - STORE
X - SERVICES
- CRAFT
△ - GOVERNMENT

■ - STORE
X - SERVICES
O - CRAFT
△ - GOVERNMENT

It functions now as a service and administrative center for a territory extending widely around it. The Pacific Coast to the south falls into its territory, and the mountain ranchos for at least a two-day mule ride on all sides turn to it for authority and supplies. It is only within the last decade that it has been connected with the rest of Mexico by anything but mule trails. Now there is a "highway." It is a road by which trucks can supply the goods from the manufacturing towns of central Mexico.

There is a good deal of optimism about, and some development of, commercial agriculture on the coast within the territory of Arteaga. As the best pass in the Coastal Mountains is on the road controlled by Arteaga, it seems likely that growth of population and prosperity on the coast will be reflected in the town.

Its street pattern is that of a grid with minor exceptions. This may indicate lateness of settlement. It is probable that it was laid out officially in the nineteenth century just before the time of its first appearance in the official record. There is no reason to believe it existed in the sixteenth century, and after the sixteenth century it is probable that new settlements were few until late in the colonial period. The few that sprang up between the early seventeenth century and the nineteenth century may have all tended to be formless (like Purépero). In the nineteenth century, due to almost total destruction of many old settlements, the consciousness of the advantage of a town plan is indicated by the re-establishment of towns in the form of the grid.

The nineteenth century "establishment" of Arteaga (previously called Carrizal) may also be shown by the fact that, although the grid was used as its pattern, it fails to carry out the sixteenth century instructions of the Spanish Government with regard to the position of the church and the administration buildings. Instead of being in positions of "honor" on the plaza, they are shunted to one side. The church is on the highest point of the town. This may indicate an attempt to meet early instructions.[4] But, the administrative offices are in positions indicating that they are of less importance than the retail stores which occupy most of the space on the plaza.[5] These stores are prosperous and the most prosperous of all are the drygoods stores.

---

[4]Dan Stanislawski, "Early Spanish Town Planning in the New World," in *The Geographical Review*, Vol. XXXVII, No. 1, 1947, p. 104.
[5]Actually the two "government" offices on the plaza are public services. One is the Post Office and the other the National Telegraph Office.

The anatomy map shows typical Hispanic concentration of activities near the plaza. Most and the best stores of town are here. Here also are the best homes of town, and the quality diminishes in almost exact proportion to distance from the plaza except along the arterials. One of these arterials meets the route to the coast; the other leads to Uruapan. There is an obvious extension of activities along these streets.

The importance of mule-driving is shown in the anatomy by the importance of activities devoted to it. Of the ten enterprises that might be termed "services," five are shelters for mules and mule-drivers. The tiny "restaurant" purveys to the drivers almost exclusively. The three barbers derive part of their trade from them.

Only that sink of iniquity, the pool hall, is solely for the use of local inhabitants. Mule-drivers contribute little to it. They are usually models of deportment. The *meson*, the "inn" for mules and their drivers, is one of the best buildings in town and is on the main route just off the plaza.

The houses are typical of Hispanic Michoacán, having adobe walls that have been plastered and calcimined. The roofs are usually of tile. A typical feature is that of the carved eaves.

Crafts are weak in Arteaga. Perhaps it is an indication of its youth in town development. Such crafts as do exist are Hispanic. For example, the most important craft group is that of leather goods. The five places of leatherworking are clearly dominant over the three woodworkers. All of the leatherworkers are either near the plaza or on one of the arterials. The woodworkers, who are repairmen rather than craftsmen, are in inferior positions.

The Balsas Lowland

This is a tectonic depression set apart sharply from the hill lands to the north and south of it. It was submerged during most of the Cretaceous and elevated only at the end of the Mesozoic. During the latter Cretaceous and early Cenozoic the southern physiographic limits were established by the elevation of the Coastal Mountains and extensions therefrom. The northern limits were more recently completed by the extrusion of young volcanic materials.[6]

This great depressed block extends from the interior of the State of Guerrero westward, along the courses of the Balsas and Tepalcatepec rivers, beyond the western border of Michoacán. Through most of its length it has a lateral extent of about fifty to seventy-five miles, but at each end it tapers to canyons between the constricting hills.

This is the Tierra Caliente (mostly Köppen BSh), an area without frost at any time of the year and, excepting the northern deserts, with the highest summer mean temperature of any part of Mexico. Its average winter temperatures are higher than those of any other part of Mexico except for a narrow strip of coast in Chiapas. The yearly range is slight, with a difference between the

---

[6] Ramiro Robles Ramos, "Orogenesis de la República Mexicana en Relación a su Relieve Actual," in *Irrigación en México*, V. 23, No. 3, May–June, 1942, pp. 42–44.

highest and lowest monthly means of only 6+°C. (Apatzingán January mean 25.3°C; May, 31.6°C.)[7]

The rains are confined almost completely to the summer season. They start here later than in other parts of the state, sometimes not until July. They continue into September. In almost all years there are six months without moisture and two more with negligible rainfall.

This is obviously a problem area for agriculture. The total figure for precipitation (Apatzingán, 28½") cannot be compared with the northern areas of the state due to the high rate of evaporation and the great yearly variation. Planting is always a hazard. It cannot take place, under ordinary circumstances, until the onset of the rains. With the shortness of the period of precipitation crops are unsuccessful in many years.

The natural vegetation is a deciduous thorn-scrub complex quite similar to that of the Coastal Mountains, including a great variety of leguminous shrubs plus a scattering of tropical fruits. These make a spiny landscape of leafless, green-gray, dead-looking branches during the long period of drought, which burst into sudden leaf and quickly transform themselves into dense verdure with the onset of the rains.

More land is included within this area than in any other region of the state, about one-third of the total. But the population is only slightly more than one-tenth of the state total. It is poor satisfaction that it appears to advantage statistically in comparison with the Coastal Mountain region. Its population density is twice that of the Coastal Mountains.

It is a region of great haciendas. Some of these, the properties with flowing water, have been expropriated by the government and parcelled out to *ejidatarios*. Other large haciendas are still in the hands of individual owners. These, for the most part, are those fit only for grazing and incapable of supporting the agriculture of *ejidatarios*. It is impossible to determine or estimate the amount of land still in the hands of hacendados. In any event, it is not of great importance in the total economy of the region.

The Balsas Lowland, like the Coastal Mountains (but less in degree) is dominated by cattle and hog economy. The area lays claim to a quarter of the state totals. Pastoral pursuits and sub-

---

[7]Alfonso Contreras Arias, *Mapa de las provincias climatológicas de la República Mexicana*, 24.

A Vaquero of the Balsas Lowland
Note leather cape and headpiece worn as protection against spines of the brush.

sistence planting fully occupy the overwhelming majority of the inhabitants. The area feeds itself, but poorly. The production of maize per hectare is only half that of the average for the state as a whole.

A little income is derived from commercial agriculture. Virtually all of the sesame raised in the state is from this lowland, most of the rice, some bananas, and a little sugar on the bordering slopes. Cascalote pods and bark (Caesalpinia Coriaria) are gathered for export to the northern tanning plants.

Plans have been made to further the development of agriculture by the use of irrigation. At present only 1 per cent of the
total land of the area is irrigated (about 7 per cent of the cultivated area). Unfortunately both the Balsas and its tributary,
the Tepalcatepec, flow too far below the surface of the land in most
places for this to be feasible.

There are three settlement types in the region. Most of the
population lives in ranchos varying in size from two or three huts
to two or three dozen. A smaller proportion of the population lives
in somewhat larger agglomerations that sprawl in amorphous

A Rancho in the Balsas Lowland

fashion over the plain. These may count their inhabitants by the
hundreds, but even so they are merely large ranchos, for town
functions, properly speaking, are lacking. A very small part of the
population is found in settlements that may be called towns. The
largest of these, although technically a "city," had a population
of less than twenty-three hundred in 1940.

Apatzingán

Near the western end of the Balsas Depression, on the banks of a little stream that contributes to the great tributary of the Balsas, the Tepalcatepec, Apatzingán is situated. It is an old settlement predating the Conquest by the Spaniards, although it is probable that the site has been changed since then.[8]

Apatzingán was of small importance when first known by Spaniards. In their early reports it was often neglected or omitted. When noted it was designated as "subject" to Tancítaro, a presently unimportant town several miles away.[9] But by reason of its position, it has had local importance during all known periods of time and through various changes in the economy of the general region. Under Indian dominance it seems to have served as a local trade center. It grew to somewhat greater importance under the Spanish colonial administration when, at first, it functioned as the local commercial center for the sugar and cacao haciendas encircling it.[10] Many of these haciendas proved to be less profitable and the region less attractive than the owners had originally hoped. After a transition period the sugar and cacao were replaced by cattle. Since that time its usefulness as a gathering and distributing point for the surrounding territory has continued. It serves the cattle ranches of the hot bottom land and those of the Coastal Ranges.

Through three centuries of colonial rule and through most of the republican period, Apatzingán was a far-off town connected with the rest of Mexico by long mule trails. With the advent of the truck,[11] the importance and function of Apatzingán is being altered. This first became notable in the 1930's.

Roads were bad at best and seemingly impossible at worst, but little daunts Mexican drivers. They pierced their way through the thorny growth and over the cobbly surface and even up the inner slopes of the Coastal Mountains. At first this meant commercial decline for Apatzingán, as its former satellite towns were supplied directly from larger cities.

---

[8]Isabel Kelly, *Excavations at Apatzingán, Michoacán*, 21–28.

[9]Descripción de Tancítaro hecha de orden de su corregidor Sebastián Macarro, a 27 de Septiembre de 1580, p. 4. MS., The University of Texas, Latin-American Collection.

[10]It was probably formally laid out in the sixteenth century. The Indians that had inhabited the pre-Conquest village were, apparently, absorbed or taken elsewhere, for its Indian character was lost at the outset.

[11]This may prove to be the most revolutionary single factor in the alteration of the urban pattern in Latin America.

Now another change has taken place. The railroad from Urua-pan has been completed to Apatzingán. It is too early to say what the ultimate effect of this will be. It seems likely, however, that the sanguine hopes of the merchants of Apatzingán will, in part at least, be fulfilled. The town will probably prosper as a rail serv-ice center.

Consideration of its anatomy indicates that the town is a mix-ture of things. It would be difficult to point to strong character of any kind. For example, the colonial Hispanic emphasis upon prestige by proximity to the plaza and arterials remains. The stores in such locations are thriving. The best houses of town have this distribution also. With increasing distance from the plaza or from the arterials the quality of both stores and houses diminishes. On the plaza or on the blocks that touch the plaza most homes are made up of several rooms around a patio. Near the edge of town, away from the arterials most homes consist of one enclosed room for sleeping in rainy weather plus several lean-tos around the patio.

The extension of importance along the arterials harks back to the days of the importance of mule-driving. Testifying also to the former importance of mule-driving in Apatzingán is the fact that most of the best stores on the plaza are now owned by men from Cotija, a town in Michoacán famous for its mule trains. The chocolate that they brought from Guatemala and the cheese that they picked up all over the Tierra Caliente became known as Chocolate of Cotija and Cheese of Cotija. Both were delivered widely through Mexico by these Spanish mule-drivers. With the decline in mule transport these energetic merchants have taken over retail stores in several towns with which they had become acquainted through their transport activities. Apatzingán was one of these.[12]

Leatherworking, which seems to be associated with Hispanic towns and mule-driving, is certainly not strongly represented, but it does account for three out of the six houses with crafts. In total, the craft activities in Apatzingán are negligible. Aside from the leatherworkers there is one metalworker, one woodworker (the necessary coffin-maker), and one tailor.

---

[12]The mule-driver is fighting a losing battle against the truck and the train. There is no longer any business for him on the slopes of the Volcanic Moun-tains that lead to the plateau of Mexico to the north. Newer transport media account for most of this. Only in the hot lowland between the narrow ribbons of roadway for truck and train and throughout most of the Coastal Mountains are there areas left to him.

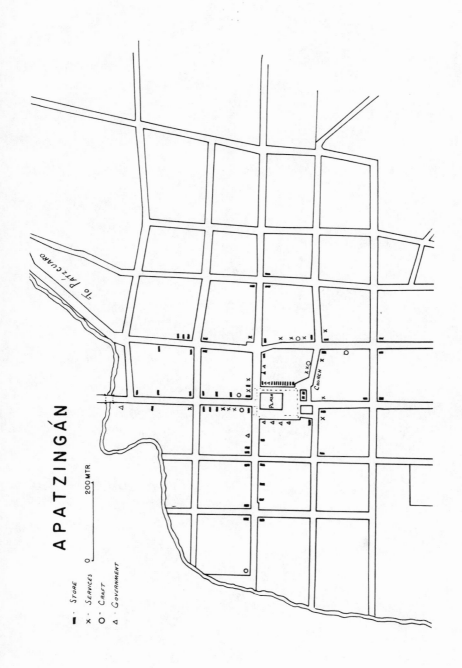

APATZINGÁN

C · CARPENTAY OR WOODWORK
T · TAILORING OR DRESSMAKING
M · METALWORK
L · LEATHERWORK
Ⓛ · TANNERY

The wars of the early nineteenth century, virtually destroyed Apatzingán. It has been put together again because a settlement in approximately this site is necessary. But due to chaotic political conditions and the changing economic situation in the Lowland, it has not re-established a definite character. The anatomy indicates little creative activity in the town. Not only have the Hispanic colonial crafts and activities largely been lost,[13] but its subsequent additions are tawdry services.

---

[13] In 1789 the colonial administration listed for Apatzingán: 2 carpenters, 4 tailors, 4 shoemakers, 4 metalworkers, 8 weavers of cotton cloth and "various women making rebozos." (See Archivo General de la Nación (AGN), *Ramo de História*, Vol. 73, Exp. 18, p. 169.)

Apatzingán seems to represent an amorphous transition stage. It retains a few of the colonial qualities, but some of its newly acquired traits clash with the old. Its services include a *meson,* the last remnant of the mule traffic, two "hotels," a boarding house, a moving picture theater, a photographic studio, four barbers, and two pool halls. These are a miscellaneous lot to be superimposed upon an old Hispanic town.

The church is along one side of the plaza, but it does not face the plaza. Its position is not such as to give it prestige as the early colonial government insisted. The biggest of the two pool halls is next to it, hardly increasing its "grandeur."

The tannery is on the edge of town but not downstream as the colonial instructions demanded. Much of the town water is taken from the stream below the tannery.

Administration has a position of unusual importance. All of one side of the plaza, some of the most important locations of the city, is occupied by administrative (largely military) offices. This is due to the strategic advantage in the position of Apatzingán. This was clearly demonstrated during the wars of the nineteenth century when it was a key military center. In a chronically uneasy political situation this function has not been lost.

Buena Vista

Buena Vista lies to the west of Apatzingán on a small tributary of the Tepalcatepec. Its site is one with good water supply and level land. Although the record of its establishment is lacking (or at least I have been unable to find it after considerable search), it is probably one of the grid pattern towns founded in the nineteenth century. Velasco[14] lists it as a "tenencia" of Tepalcatepec in 1890. Presumably it was quite small as he does not give a population for it. In 1900 the census credits it with a population of 212, and its official status is that of "pueblo." In 1940 the census shows a population of 927.

Its importance is recent, of this century, and is a product of trucking. Its growth has reflected the growing importance of the motor truck and contrasts with the decline in other towns of the area which formerly prospered by mule driving. It is a service center for trucks. From Buena Vista they carry merchandise to Aguililla in the Coastal Mountains and to ranchos and small settlements on the slopes and in the Balsas valley.

---

[14]Alfonso Luis Velasco, *Geografía y Estadística de la República Mexicana,* Tomo VI, p. 151.

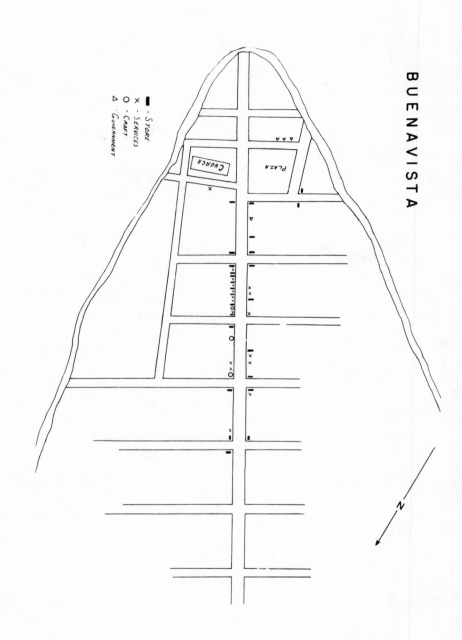

BUENAVISTA

■ - Store
× - Services
○ - Craft
△ - Government

CHURCH

PLAZA

N

It is actually a one-street town. This may indicate the difference in a settlement developed for truckers from one established
by mule drivers. The tortuous streets of Purépero which were
formed presumably by the erratic course of mules, around boul-
ders, trees, etc., are quite different from the straight main street
that serves as a truckers' service center.

BUENAVISTA

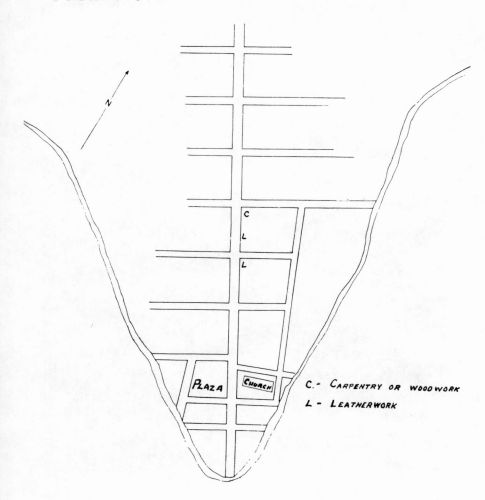

C. - CARPENTRY OR WOODWORK

L - LEATHERWORK

There is a plaza with several government offices on it. There is also a church. Both the plaza and the church are situated at one end of town and are offside in terms of activities. They are, likewise, situated at the lower end, which is considered to be the least healthy.

The number of services is disproportionately high. The pool halls, saloons, boarding houses, restaurants, and warehouses all serve the business of the truckers.

There are virtually no crafts. This may be an indication of youth as it seems to be in Arteaga. Like this latter place such crafts as exist are those that seem to be essential to an Hispanic settlement. There are two shoemakers and one repair carpenter. The two shoemakers are in or near the block of greatest concentration of activities. The carpenter is slightly farther out.

Churumuco

Churumuco

Churumuco, the hottest and perhaps the most miserable of all Michoacán pueblos, was aboriginal.[15] It has had as long a record of little importance as any settlement in Michoacán, but it has been persistent.

In the hot valley of the Balsas, it is situated upon a terrace about a half mile distant from the river. Encircled by mountains, the hot temperatures of the Tierra Caliente are unrelieved by breezes.

For a full day's mule ride on the trail from the north, before arriving at Churumuco hardly a habitation is to be seen. In such a spiny, drought-limited country there seems to be little reason for a settlement. But all things are relative. There are people scattered through the brush of the surrounding mountains. A local service center is needed, and Churumuco has certain advantages above other sites in the area. Water flows in the arroyo near the town until December and can be taken out with buckets. After December shallow holes can be dug into the arroyo bottom, and by increasing their depth water is available until the onset of the rains.

There is little of interest in the town anatomy. Specialized activities are few. The government offices are on the plaza. The church is established in approved fashion on the highest point in town and set back in its yard so that it is properly "honored." The trade such as exists is handled almost entirely by the three stores at the plaza. Two other tiny ones hardly deserve the name.

The grid of the present town is completely regular. This probably dates only from the last half of the nineteenth century. Local inhabitants speak of a formless town in the time of their grandparents. They also speak of the church that was then a mere "jacal" with a thatched roof. Undoubtedly the town is one of the nineteenth century re-establishments. It is similar in this to Ário de Rosales and Arteaga. It serves as a small service center for ranchos and a newly developing commercial agriculture based on sesame and coconuts.

---

[15]*Relación de las ceremonias y ritas y población y governación de los Indios de la provincia de Michuacan hecha al illmo. Señor Don Antonio de Mendoza virrey y governador de esta Nueva España por S.M. (?) G.*, 288. (Commonly known as *Relación de Michoacán*.)

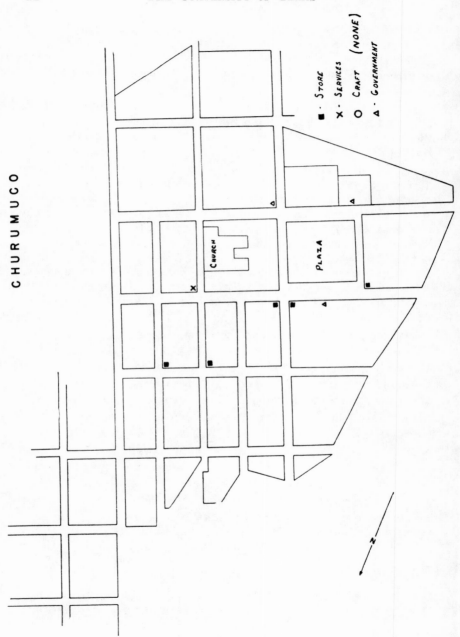

The main store in Churumuco

The Transition Zone

Upslope from the Balsas depression, on the southern flank of the Volcanic Mountains between 1,500 and 2,000 M. elevation is the Tierra Templada. It is the narrow zone of moderate temperatures and rainfall forming the transition between the hot, baked Balsas Lowland and the cooler mountain slopes and valleys to the north.

In the Köppen classification the area would fall near the division line between Cwa and Cwb.[16] There are a few days of light frost in most years. Fifty inches of rainfall is average for the major settlements, almost all of it falling within the four summer months, June to September. Only occasionally are there light winter rains.

The natural vegetation reflects the midway position of the area on the mountain slope. The typical species are the live oak (Quercus harmsiana—Standley citing Trelease[17]), pines (Pinus leiophylla, P. montezumae) extending down from the higher elevations, and copal (Elaphrium jorullense) from below.

Each of the important settlements of the zone is located upon an entry (boca) to the Balsas depression. Each has a good route from the north into a section of the hot country, taps that section for its products, and in turn supplies it with manufactured goods from the outside.

The region and its settlements are favored in many ways. Its climate is excellent both for men and crops, and lying at the contact between the hot and cool lands, between the vast, relatively inaccessible spaces below and the regions of greater density of population to the north, it has developed industries for the processing of hot country raw materials for sale in the rest of the state and in other states beyond.

Very different from the two regions previously considered, this is an area of town living. More of the inhabitants here are occupied in industry, communication and transport, and commerce than those of any other area of the state. The Mexican census classes over one-third of the population in this area as "urban."

Supporting this is a prosperous agriculture. It is an area of good lands, reasonably level. There are many relatively flat surfaces, excellent for irrigation. More than a third of the cultivated land is so used. Great sugar cane plantations that have produced wealth since the sixteenth century still thrive around Tacámbaro. Coffee is exported. Maize and wheat production is normal to the population in comparison with total state figures, as are the products of grazing industries.

This is not an area typified by the subsistence rancho, which has minor importance. It is an area of commercial production. This commercial agriculture plus craft industries and commerce give character to the zone.

---

[16]Robert C. West, *Cultural Geography of the Modern Tarascan Area,* 5.
[17]Paul C. Standley, *Trees and Shrubs of Mexico,* 1649.

Ário de Rosales

At slightly under 7,000 feet elevation on the south slope of the Volcanic Mountains is a gently sloping tableland on which lies Ário de Rosales. The soils are fertile, and the relatively level fields are easily plowed. The rainfall of this Transition Slope is adequate. A few miles upslope from Ário is the spring that is the source of the stream that makes Ário and a good deal of the agriculture around it possible.

This was an Indian settlement before the Spaniards knew Mexico. It can hardly have had importance for it is mentioned only casually in the documents relating to the early sixteenth century. It may have functioned as a way-station for the Tarascan armies on their way to conquests in the Balsas Lowland and in the Coastal Mountains. That it was on a route from the Mexican Plateau to the Pacific Ocean was made known to Cortés, who sent men and equipment along the route to establish Zacatula as his headquarters for exploration along the west coast. At the end of the sixteenth century it was a "cabecera," a local administrative center, but of very modest importance.[18]

But its growth is foreshadowed. Just at the turn of the century the colonial administration was trying to redistribute population in this area. Their purpose was to establish a permanent settlement and a smelter for the copper ores from Inguarán and Churumuco. Ário was recommended highly as being a place with good water where a much larger population could be maintained, where the land was fertile, where property was not already taken up (by Spaniards) and where there was plenty of wood for making charcoal (Ário lies just at the lower edge of the pine region). The names of several small settlements were mentioned as likely prospects to be "congregated" at the site of Ário. This apparently was done.[19]

In this report it is mentioned casually that Ário lies on the Camino Real from the sea. The Manila trade had not assumed importance at that time. It later became an important factor in the growth and importance of Ário. Acapulco became the terminus of the Manila galleons, and much of their merchandise was brought

---

[18]Luis García Pimentel, *Relación de los Obispados de Tlaxcala, Michoacán, Oaxaca y otros lugares en .el siglo XVI* (Manuscrito de la colección del Señor Don Joaquín García Icazbalceta), 33.

[19]Archivo General de Indias (AGI), Audiencia de México, *Minas de Metal descubierta en Michoacán, México, 1599*, leg. 258, 60-1-41, pp. 35, 38, 40 ff.

into central Mexico along the mule trail that led up the coast almost to the mouth of the Balsas, where it turned north to cross the river at about the great bend. From there it went upslope to pass through Ário.[20]

With the establishment of the Galleon trade, a town approximately in the position of Ário was most desirable. Once established, the town spurred the development of farming around it. Before the end of the colonial period a number of large haciendas near Ário were prospering on the basis of sugar, indigo, cattle, maize, and wheat.[21]

The products of the Balsas Lowland, hides, cheese, indigo, copper, cotton, rice, and cascalote were brought into Ário increasingly during the colonial period. From there they were redistributed into other parts of Mexico.

As Ário was an unimportant village during the sixteenth century, the century of rigorous town planning, it was not formally laid out. It seems that the rigor of planning had abated by the early seventeenth century when Ário was enlarged by the addition of the other villages. From early accounts the town was then "formless."[22]

Its function after the sixteenth century was that of a mule-transport center, a Transition-slope town serving as intermediary between the hot Lowland and the uplands of central Mexico. It grew by slow but steady accretion, probably like the later Purépero, to meet the requirements of mule-drivers.

Only after its destruction in the "wars of liberation" in the early nineteenth century was it laid out according to a grid plan.[23]

---

[20] Archivo General de la Nación (AGN), *Ramo de História*, Vol. 73, Expediente 18, p. 213.

[21] AGN, *Ramo de História*, Vol. 73, Expediente 18, p. 212.

[22] It was recorded in 1789 that the town was "beginning to put order in its pattern of streets." AGN, *Ramo de História*, Vol. 73, Expediente 18, p. 214.

[23] José Guadalupe Romero, *Noticias para formar la historia y la estadística del Obispado de Michoacán, México*, 137.

The ordered pattern of streets in New World settlements was begun in the early decades of the sixteenth century (see Stanislawski, "Early Spanish Town Planning in the New World," in *The Geographical Review*, Vol. XXXVII, No. 1, 1947, pp. 95–105) but for remote settlements or those that sprang up quickly, like mining cities, the idea was not strictly enforced. Zacatecas is perhaps a good example of this. It was founded just before the middle of the century, after many "ordered" towns had been established. It was far away, however, and developed quickly. There is a suggestion of the grid but with many flaws.

Between the time of the founding of Zacatecas and the end of the century was the time of the rigorous insistence upon careful and precise establishments. San Luis Potosí, another city founded because of mining but over a

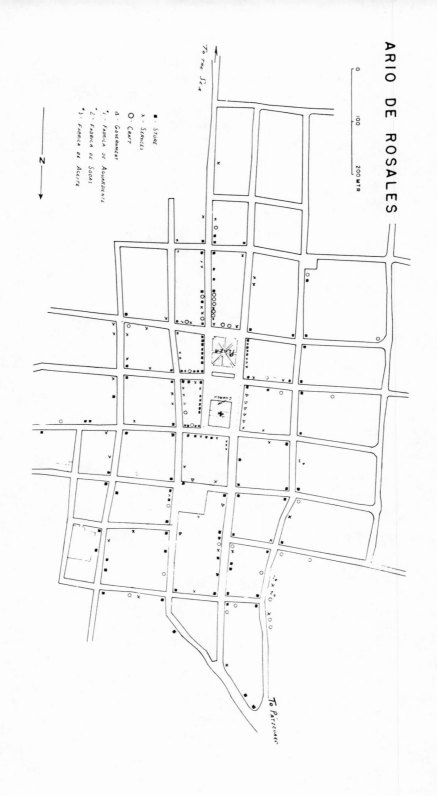

ARIO DE ROSALES

■ - STORE
× - SERVICES
○ - CRAFT
△ - GOVERNMENT
¹ - FABRICA DE AGUARDIENTE
² - FABRICA DE SODAS
³ - FABRICA DE ACEITE

N

0   100   200 MTR

To THE SEA

To PATZCUARO

The few Indians that were congregated here in the early seventeenth century were quickly pushed out or absorbed into the growing mestizo settlement. It has long been mestizo in blood and cultural quality.

The anatomy of the present town reflects its background and the continuing importance of its intermediate position and exchange function between the hot and moderate lands. It is the outlet for the part of the Balsas Valley to the south of it and for a considerable part of the Pacific Coast of the State of Guerrero. Through it pass the hides and cheese of the cattle industry of the Lowland, the sesame, part of which is pressed in a small oil plant in Ário and most of the remainder shipped into larger towns for processing, the cascalote, which is shipped on to the shoe manufacturing centers.

It is a bustling place, perhaps the most energetically commercial in all of Michoacán. It is efficient in its dealings. Business is the "way of life" and the inhabitants work at commerce in such a way as to make them unique among the towns studied.

It is surprising that there is no more industry in town. Ário has been a commercial center for three and a half centuries, and yet transport and exchange is its real function and the processing of materials is relatively unimportant. The small oil plant processes but a small part of the sesame that is carried into Ário from the Lowland. Floor mats are made from palm leaves in one very small plant but most of the palm leaves are carried through Ário to Tarascan mountain villages where they are the raw material of a hat industry. The most notable item of their manufacture is the "riata" or rope made from the fibres of the maguey plant. This is an old and honorable craft. The riata is famous among mule-drivers, and what is honored among mule-drivers may well be assumed to be honorable in Ário.

The anatomy map shows a great concentration around the plaza. The greatest number of activities are here and also the most pros-

---

generation later than Zacatecas, is almost a perfect example of the grid. Up until the end of the century, when there were the general instructions as to "congregations," this insistence upon careful layout was continued. It is probable that shortly after the end of the century this insistence lessened. This was reasonable in view of the fact that the "congregating" was virtually complete. There were few towns formed after that time. Those that did come into being were allowed to grow according to their own tastes until the early nineteenth century. Then again, due to destruction in the wars, many towns had to be re-established and a master plan was needed. As in the early sixteenth century, the grid was chosen.

Ário de Rosales

Market in Ário de Rosales

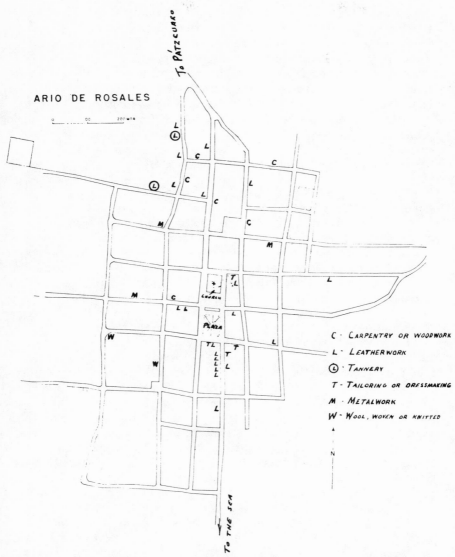

ARIO DE ROSALES

C - CARPENTRY OR WOODWORK
L - LEATHERWORK
Ⓛ - TANNERY
T - TAILORING OR DRESSMAKING
M - METALWORK
W - WOOL, WOVEN OR KNITTED

perous. This concentration is even greater than appears on the map, for there is a daily market with energetic exchange of perishable foods and other materials that takes place in the plaza and on the nearby streets.

The main street of town, which runs to the west of the plaza and the two adjacent streets (the one to the east is slightly offset) show the extension of activities (and values) toward the north where they converge to meet the overland route into Pátzcuaro. To the south of the plaza only one street shows an extension of activities. This leads to the route into the Balsas Lowland. Stores have appropriated most of the corner positions along the arterials.

Crafts are not as strong in Ário as one might expect. It is probably a result of their centuries-old devotion to commerce to the exclusion of almost everything else. In comparison with Tacámbaro, its sister city of the Transition slope, its crafts make a poor showing.

As should be expected, leathergoods follow stores in positional importance. They are particularly concentrated on the southern arterial. They seem to be associated with mesones which is not surprising. There are a few near the plaza and others, including two tanning centers, near the junction of streets leading to the Pátzcuaro route. Tailors appear to be well respected, although the number is small. Carpenters—repairmen here as in the other Hispanic towns—are few and tend to be in inferior locations. Weavers and metalworkers are obviously inferior—virtual outcasts. Administrative offices are in preferred sites.

The church has the position that was probably assigned to it at an early time. As is the case in Purépero, the church is placed well with regard to the plaza, but it is not set back in a large yard "so that it might have greater honor." The commercial citizens of Ário, like the same type in Purépero, are "not very Catholic" as they say themselves. Thus they do not go to any lengths to maintain the dominance of the church, although they do accord it the position in a settlement demanded by Iberian authority.

The *mesones* of Ário are found in relatively good positions. Several are located in the blocks adjacent to the plaza.

From early accounts, the pine forests around Ário were luxuriant. It was mostly for this reason that the congregation of the early seventeenth century was made in this place. The pine was converted into charcoal for use in the smelting process and the depletion of the forests began at that time. Probably the result was not too serious for there is no record of problems resulting from deforestation during the colonial or early republican period. Real trouble was caused at the end of the nineteenth century when the little narrow-gauge railway was established, and this woodburner effectively stripped the hills nearby. For the last generation Ário has increasingly faced the problem of water supply.

Ário once had sugar haciendas near it, as has been the case with its companion city Tacámbaro, since early in the colonial period, but Ário is situated about 1,300 feet higher on the slope than Tacámbaro. It lies just at the boundary of the Cwa and Cwb climates, at the cool fringe of sugar production. Tacámbaro has a clear advantage in this respect.

The continuing "plantation economy" of Tacámbaro as opposed to the "commercial economy" of Ário is to be understood partly in terms of history and partly in terms of temperatures and flowing water.

Tacámbaro

Tacámbaro is fully within the Cwa climate of the temperate southern slope, the transition zone between the hot Balsas Lowland and the Volcanic Mountains to the north. Its choice as a place of settlement by sixteenth century Spaniards and its persistent function are to be understood primarily in terms of this position.

There are not many good routes from the low hot valley and coast to the central plateau of Mexico. Tacámbaro lies on one of these routes. Its site has the advantage of good water supply for the uses of the settlement, but, more than this, it is sufficient to irrigate the relatively level and fertile lands that were recognized at the outset as promising for agriculture.

Cristobal de Oñate was one of the leaders of the Spanish Conquest. We may assume that his choice of the Tacámbaro region for his encomienda was a testimony to its obvious value. It included gently rolling land of volcanic soils that proved to be excellent for sugar cane. The mild climate with fifty inches of rainfall plus irrigation water produced wealth virtually from the outset. It was not only a matter of excellence for agriculture that made it desirable. It is recorded that the charm and beauty of the location impressed the hard-bitten conquistador and was part of his reason for selection.

Judging by the lack of emphasis put upon the settlement in the only document treating with the pre-Spanish Tarascan settlements,[24] it may be supposed that it was not a place of importance to the Tarascans. It is improbable that they used the Tacámbaro

---

[24] *Relación de Michoacán.*

route to the Lowland.[25] But it was not long, certainly, after the Spanish assumed control that traffic was established.

The eastern section of the Balsas Lowland, where the states of Michoacán and Guerrero meet, has been a region of relatively dense population since long before the Conquest. There were large and prosperous settlements there with which the Tarascans had traded and which were ultimately conquered by them.

The Augustinians chose Tacámbaro as the starting place from which to launch their campaign in the hot Lowland. Officially their "university"[26] and center was in Tiripitío, but Oñate invited them to use Tacámbaro as a headquarters for this work and they accepted. The "university" was moved to Tacámbaro in 1545 and then it became officially the center of Augustinian activity in the Balsas Valley.[27]

For several generations Tacámbaro was the slope town of greatest importance in this area. It functioned as an intermediary between central Mexico and the hot country for both tradesmen and ecclesiastics. Spanish or mestizo mule-drivers started from here for either the large settlements to the southeast or the longer journey toward the south-southwest to the great bend of the Balsas and from there to the coast.[28] Coming from the Tierra Caliente, they converged upon Tacámbaro and then fanned out along several routes into the central highlands and plateau of Mexico.

In the middle of the sixteenth century a population of nearly two thousand in the general vicinity was distributed among three pueblos and several smaller units.[29] At the end of the century it was suggested that the smaller places should be abandoned and the population moved to this center. This apparently was carried out, for the names of the little settlements disappear from the record.

In 1620 the Counts of Oñate were thriving in the possession of their sugar estates, operated mainly with Indian labor but also with imported Negro slaves.[30]

---

[25]Dan Stanislawski, "Tarascan Political Geography," in *American Anthropologist*, Vol. 49, No. 1, Jan.–March, 1947.

[26]Their university was founded in 1540 as perhaps the first university in the New World. It was designed to function as a training center for Augustinians going to work in the hot Lowland. See Diego Basalenque, *Historia de la Provincia de San Nicolás de Tolentino de Michoacán, del Orden de N.P.S. Augustín*, I, 163, *et seq.*

[27]Jesús Romero Flores, *Tacámbaro*, 33.

[28]Basalenque, *op. cit.*, 93 *et seq.*

[29]Francisco del Paso y Troncoso, *Papeles de Nueva España. Segundo Serie, Geografía y estadística*, I, 252.

[30]Biblioteca Nacional, Madrid, *Relación of the Bishopric of Michoacán*, 1620, Sept. 20. Original Bib. Palacio, Madrid in MS. 2579, 24 ff. (unnumbered), Catálogo No. 267, Vol. 11.

TACÁMBARO

0   100   200 MTR

■ - STORE
X - SERVICES
O - CRAFT
▲ - GOVERNMENT
#1 - SUGAR WHSE.
#2 - MARKET - BROADS THROUGHOUT BLOCK
#3 - SESAME WHSE.
#4 - CASCALOTE WHSE.
#5, 6, 8, 9 - FÁBRICA DE SODAS
#7 - FÁBRICA DE AGUARDIENTE
#10 SUGAR MILL

PLAZA

CHURCH

To Ario
To Pátzcuaro
To Chupio
To Balsas Valley
To Balsas Valley
To Pátzcuaro
Mountain Settlements

N

A half century later an Augustinian reported that it remained one of the most beautiful and fruitful places on earth and that it still was the entryway for Augustinians into the *Tierra Caliente* as well as serving the same function for the mule trains.[31]

A report on Tacámbaro in 1748 gives the population in terms of races. The Indians were fewer. They accounted for less than half of the families in the town, although their total was still greater than either that of the Spaniards or Negroes.[32] The sugar estates and factories continued to prosper greatly.

The tradesmen and craftsmen of Tacámbaro also did well until the Creole revolution in the early nineteenth century. The warm slope and the scattered towns of the hot Lowlands suffered greatly at that time. Tacámbaro was badly damaged, her population partly scattered, the prosperous stores and craftsmen temporarily put out of business.[33] But it was only temporary, for the value of the lands and position of Tacámbaro are such that a settlement there is mandatory. By the end of the nineteenth century Tacámbaro was functioning in much the same way that it had in previous times. Its sugar estates and factories—the most important still in the hands of the Counts of Oñate—were doing well. Its stores and its craftsmen were operating in much the same way and with the same type of articles. The mule trains from the south continued as important even though Ário had appropriated virtually all of the trade of the "Costa Grande," the ancient route that crossed the Balsas near its great bend. The eastern Balsas region, however, looked to Tacámbaro as its link with central Michoacán and part of Mexico beyond.

By this time the Indians were almost all gone. Either they had been pushed into other locations, or they had been absorbed into a mestizo group. The Negroes likewise had been absorbed. Tacámbaro, in the twentieth century, is mestizo.

Tacámbaro was established by Spaniards as a planned unit. This is clear from the fact that it was a planned grid. There are slight exceptions to its regularity that may have existed from the beginning. More likely, they came into being gradually.

The Counts of Oñate and other Spaniards who took land here put their stamp on the settlement. Its quality, as a center for land-

<hr>

[31] Basalenque, *op. cit.*, 163 *et seq.*
[32] D. Antonio de Villaseñor y Sánchez, *Parte que Corresponde a Michoacán en la estadística que con el nombre de TEATRO AMERICANO . . .*, 12.
[33] Juan José Martínez de Lejarza, *Análisis estadístico de la Provincia de Michuacan*, 120–121.

holding families, is different from that of the other towns of the warm slope. More than this, it had advantages because of its priority. Ário strove for long generations before it took over the control of the mule route to the Costa Grande in spite of its superior position relative to that route. In the matter of crafts, Tacámbaro's advantage is clearer. It started in upon and developed those particular Hispanic crafts that are associated with mule-driving. It still shows advantages in the leather crafts.

Tacámbaro has more similarity to Pátzcuaro than to any other of the settlements considered in this paper. It is fair to assume that this is partly due to their similarity of function with regard

The Plaza in Tacámbaro

to landholding families and their attitude toward life. The atmosphere of the plaza in Tacámbaro is more like that of Pátzcuaro than that of Ário, its slope companion. The pace of the people is more leisurely. One feels the bustle of the commercial activity in the plaza of Ário. Not so, Tacámbaro. In fact, there is very little market activity in Tacámbaro. The Hispanic attitude toward certain crafts is obvious in the distribution. Shoemakers are nu-

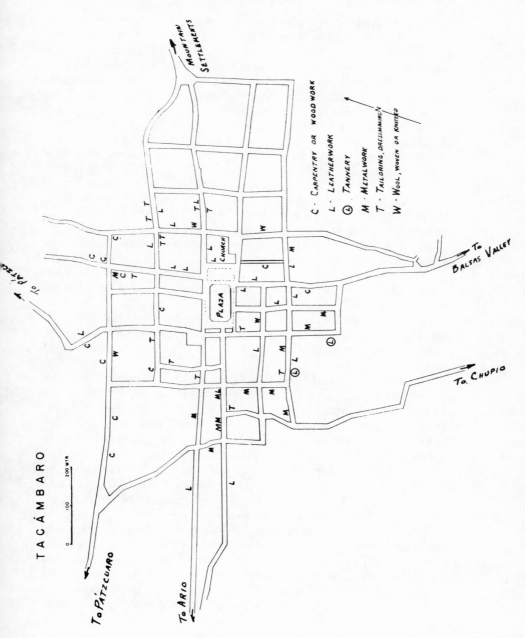

merous, and they hold a better average position that that of any other craft. The other types of leather goods stand in second best position in town. Metalworkers are in poorer locations. The worst position is occupied by the weavers and the carpenters.

The carpenters make almost no furniture. They are repairmen, but more importantly they are the coffinmakers. If it is not a highly respected craft, it at least is sustained by a steady demand.

The hides for its leather crafts come in from the hot country to the southeast. They are cured with cascalote from the same region. The making of shoes and huaraches is the most important leather craft, but belts and leather parts of the saddles and leather thongs are important. And highly important are the gloves (made either of cowhide or deerskin) to protect the hands of the vaqueros against the lariats made of maguey fibre. Without a thick cover of leather on his hand such a rope would tear the flesh cruelly.

Also the palms on the hot lower slopes serve as raw material for the crafts of Tacámbaro. Part of the trunk is used to make the sweat pads for the backs of the burros. Long ropes for staking out the burros at night are made from palm fibre. Whips for the use of mule-drivers are made from the fronds.

Obviously Tacámbaro does not use all of the products of the hot country that are transported by the mule-drivers. Cattle, hides, hogs, cascalote, and other items are taken through the plateau of Mexico.

Tacámbaro is a clean, well-kept, comfortable looking town. Its houses are kept in neat order for the most part. Most of them are frequently and carefully calcimined. Most of them have the wide, carved eaves that represent an import from Europe but have been lengthened and elaborated in the last two centuries by mestizos in Michoacán. Virtually all have roofs of tile. There are four hotels in Tacámbaro, a disproportionately high number for the size of the town, although the largest has but ten rooms. They are clean and well run. One of them even has a shower. Most streets of the town are well cobbled and kept in good shape.

The market of Tacámbaro is of little importance. It probably was once more important than now, while the Indian population remained. But with the Indians gone from the vicinity, the permanent commercial establishments supply all of the needs of the mestizo permanent and transient population. The most prosperous of the permanent commercial establishments clearly are the dry-goods stores.

The house distribution in terms of quality is typical for the Hispanic town. The most valuable property and the best houses are on the plaza or on the blocks that touch the plaza. There is a slightly greater extension of the best quality houses to the north than to the south. Men of the town agreed that it was so although they had no quick answer for it. It was suggested that the upper

Home near the edge of Tacámbaro

part of town was cooler, had more breeze, and also there was "more movement." That is, the main route to Pátzcuaro was on that side and so commercial activity would be more brisk. The subconscious realization that a place of commercial advantage is a preferred residential site was thus expressed.

Activities, store, crafts and services are more widely spread in Tacámbaro than in Ário, or indeed, than in any other of the Hispanic towns. The explanation is not clear. It is probably due to the complexity of the events and processes that created the settlement and have contributed to its four centuries of life and development.

It has long been a center of landholding families. It has never had an important market function. Its crafts and transport facilities are age-old. In some ways the combination of these has brought about a greater degree of activity and a greater dispersal of it. Notwithstanding this, it is clearly Hispanic. The blank spaces on the anatomy map are notably the areas not associated with the plaza or the main routes. For example, the east end of town and the mid-block locations on those streets not conducing the main cross-country routes.

The *mesones* are in locations of prestige. Most of them are near the plaza and among the first quality homes.

The Volcanic Mountain Region

This is a topographically complex highland, a part of the great transverse mountain system extending across middle Mexico. In Michoacán it lies between the parallels of 19° and 20° north latitude.

The average height of the southern part of the great Mexican plateau is here increased by the masses of volcanic materials heaped upon it. The vulcanism is recent. Parícutin born within this decade stands now more than 1700 feet higher than the corn field from which it started. But the vulcanism has had a long period of activity. It is probable that it has been active since early Tertiary, producing a highly varied relief consisting of composite volcanoes, cinder cones, and lava flows.[34] Elevations of the peaks reach the maximum in western Michoacán of 12,660 feet in Mt. Tancítaro. Towns of the area vary in elevation from over 5,000 feet to almost 8,500 feet.

The most typical features of the landscape, the Tertiary volcanic cones show to varying degrees the erosive effect of radial drainage upon the andesite that makes up the greater part of the material on their flanks. More numerous are the smaller quaternary cinder cones. They are composed mostly of semi-consolidated ash, cinder, and large explosion remnants.

The basalt that flowed from breaches in the sides of old volcanoes has covered considerable expanses of territory, and the degree of its disintegration is directly related to the age of the deposit. The older flows now support a sparse vegetation; the younger are raw infertile blots on the landscape and an obstacle to communications.

The disintegration and erosion of these various volcanic materials has resulted in numerous small intermontane alluvial basins.

---

[34]For a discussion of this and the region in general see West, *op. cit.*

In most cases their fertility is high, although reduced by the porosity of their volcanic constituents.

Most of this area falls into the Cwb classification, according to the Köppen system, with the highest slopes being Cwc. The summers are moderately warm with winters somewhat less so. The annual range is nowhere great. Frosts are common, however, at night from November to March. Due to differences in elevations and exposures, one valley or settlement may show considerable variation from another.

Precipitation comes mostly in the four-month period of June to September as a result of convection during the summer. A small part of the precipitation falls outside of the four-month period. There are occasional drizzles and light winter rains, probably of cyclonic origin. The total precipitation for the region as a whole would average about 30 inches but with notable variations according to local conditions. For example, Pátzcuaro records an average of 44 inches, almost as much as falls in the Transition Zone.

The dominant vegetation of the mountain zone is pine-oak. (There are several species, the chief examples of which are Pinus leiophylla, used commonly for turpentine, and the P. michoacana var. cornuta, used for lumber.) Several species of oak, both deciduous and persistent, occur, the commonest species being Quercus fulva and Q. acuminata. Often mixed with the pine and oak are the madroño (Arbutus sp.) and various "laurels." A number of epiphytes appear on the branches of the trees.

The oaks appear in greatest numbers in the lower parts of the forest. At higher elevations the proportion of pines is greater, although at the highest slopes fir (Abies religiosa) dominates.

This is the most complex region of the state, complex in topography, climatic regions, vegetation, and soil regions. But more than this, the economy is complicated by the presence of sharply differing ethnic groups. This is the region of the Tarascan Indians whose villages are on the slopes and in little valleys, lying for the most part between 2,000 and 2,500 meters in elevation. There are, also, numerous mestizo settlements. The differences in attitudes and economies are readily notable. As a whole the area has endowments beyond those of the average for the state. The population density is relatively high (13 per cent of the territory of the state but 22 per cent of the population, with a density of 30/km²). This population is in direct and obvious response to the quality of soils, amount of rainfall and moderate temperatures.

Most Indian villages have adequate agricultural lands for their support. Some, indeed, are very well favored. Their production of maize and wheat per acre is relatively high. Beans and squashes are planted in the corn fields, and the Tarascan has added the European cattle and hogs. There is no suggestion of the cattle ranch here. It is a matter of family ownership of one or two—at most a few—cows per family.

To supplement their income some of the Indians have maintained certain of their ancient crafts, notably woodworking and textiles. The sheep was a welcome addition to their cool highlands, and sheep's wool long since replaced native cotton as the common textile fibre.

In the lower and larger valleys and in the best crossroads, trading centers, mestizos have either replaced the Indian or at least have become dominant.

This is an area of village and town dwelling. The rancho scarcely exists. Over a quarter of the population lives in towns designated as urban units by the census. Virtually all other persons live in villages with the form, organization, and function of towns.

"Industries" are important in the area. In Tarascan villages it is, however, "cottage" industries that are not ordinarily recorded in the census. In mestizo villages both cottage type and small factory production are present.

Trade is important. Among Indians there is a good deal of exchange of the products of their specialized crafts. These are also sold to mestizos. The mestizo towns act as centers of exchange, dealing in Indian craft articles as well as manufactured imports. It is the mestizo who handles transport.

Pichátaro

The village of Pichátaro is on a low knoll looking out over a beautiful and fertile mountain valley of approximately 8,000 feet elevation. It lies about 1,000 feet higher than Erongarícuaro and is three hours distance from it by muleback. It is high enough to lie on the border of the Cwb and Cwc climates, but the growing season is long enough for a prosperous agriculture.

There are ample lands to feed the villagers well and to produce a surplus sufficient to support a number of craftsmen who are, partly at least, producers of luxury goods.

Pichátaro has never been a large settlement. It was in existence before the arrival of the Spaniards. They altered the form of the unplanned Indian village by imposing the grid. They also added the church. But seemingly the life of the Tarascans was otherwise changed but little.

Near the end of the sixteenth century Ponce[35] found it to be a small village with water brought in to irrigate its crops. There were many fruit trees. It has grown since then, but part of his description still holds. The good springs nearby are still furnishing the water for irrigation of their lands. There are still many fruit trees. In fact, Pichátaro has started, in a small way, the commercial production of apples.[36]

We have another brief report on Pichátaro in 1788 when it was described as having well-placed houses on beautiful little streets.[37] It was completely Indian. The orchards were still notable as also fine harvests of wheat and maize. Only one craft, carpentry, was mentioned.

Pichátaro has had good luck. It has always had good lands and sufficient acreage for its population. It was sufficiently removed from contact with the Spanish landholders around Lake Pátzcuaro so that the village lands were not appropriated to be included in haciendas as was the case near the lake. Yet being situated on the route between the lake and other mountain villages farther to the west, it has not stagnated by isolation.

This explains a good deal of the quality of present Pichátaro. Its inhabitants have come in contact with other places and people. A few "foreigners" settled there, and it is no longer 100 per cent Tarascan in speech[38] but it was never made a stopping place for mule-drivers. Its location only three hours away from Erongarícuaro precluded this.

The effect of the few mestizos who have settled in town is chiefly seen in the stores. Of eleven in the village, six are owned by mestizos. This does not properly indicate their importance, how-

---

[35]Fray Alonso Ponce, *Relación breve y verdadera de algunas cosas de las muchas que sucedieron al padre Fray Alonso Ponce en las provincias de la Nueva España . . .,* II, 6.

[36]Trees are notable in all of the mountain villages of these Tarascan Indians. The appearance of the villages is often that of houses in the midst of orchards (although not commercial orchards with the trees in seried rows). This is all the more noticeable inasmuch as Hispanic towns in this area are almost treeless when viewed from the street. This may involve a difference in cultural attitude between the Spaniard and the Indian.

[37]AGN, *Ramo de História,* Vol. 73, Expediente 18, p. 100.

[38]West, *op. cit.,* Map 11, p. 16.

ever, for the mestizo stores do probably 95 per cent of the business. They are nearest to the plaza. The Tarascan stores are farther out and with one exception have nothing more in stock than a few bottles of soft drinks, a few cakes of soap, and perhaps a few candles. They are hardly businesses. Hour by hour the owner may be found sleeping, chatting, or working at odd chores without a glimpse of a customer. Toward the end of the afternoon and in the early evening when business is brisk, one or two of the mestizo stores are crowded and do a bustling business while the little Tarascan stores have only an occasional customer.

The idea of the store is somewhat alien to these Indians. They transact their business and exchange their surplus goods between one another or in the market places of Erongarícuaro and Pátzcuaro. Each Sunday several groups jog downhill to Erongarícuaro to the market. Their chief product for exchange is pine wood that they cut in the surrounding hills. In the Erongarícuaro market they meet the lake fishers, and there they barter their wood for fish. When there is a surplus of wheat or maize, and fruits in season, they also are taken to market.

All stores, mestizo and Tarascan, are located on the main street, which is the "through route." This is in keeping with Hispanic

Outskirts of Pichátaro

PICHÁTARO

B - Embroidered Blouses
C - Carpentry or Woodwork
W - Wool, Woven or Knitted
L - Leatherwork
H - Hats

practice and is due to the influence of the mestizos who have come into the town.

The anatomy of the town indicates its difference from Hispanic settlements. There is far less concentration of activities. That which does exist is due to mestizo store influence on the main street. As for Tarascan crafts, they are widely scattered and show no tendency to be near to the plaza or in any other particular part of town. As far as one can determine, there is no preferred location. There are carpenters near the plaza, on the main street as well as in the outlying blocks. The same is true of hatmakers and weavers. Position carries no prestige.

The same is true of houses. There is little difference in quality between a house on or near the plaza and a house at the outskirts. In fact, the two chief officials of town at the time that this inquiry was made lived at one extreme corner of the village. They both agreed that one place was as good as another for one's home. They had no idea of the value of a lot. They said that sales were so infrequent that it was hard to state a price. It all depended on "how much you wanted to pay."

The function of crafts within the village and the attitude of the Indians toward crafts is quite different from that in Hispanic settlements. It is non-commercial insofar as trade outside of the village is concerned. The crafts are almost all Indian and the exceptions have been fitted into an Indian pattern of use and wont. This is in spite of mestizos and their control of the main stores. It is so because crafts are partly "luxury." Tarascans of Pichátaro are fundamentally farmers who make or support the making of things for their greater comfort and satisfaction. Now crafts are not taken up commercially but to supply things that can be used in town. Only occasionally are the embroidered blouses or belts of woven wool taken into the markets. Actually, the only craft that is pursued for commercial purposes is the most ancient of their crafts, that of woodworking. But this is only one specialized part of their woodworking—that of making canoe paddles. Pichátaro, three hours away from Lake Pátzcuaro, makes most of the paddles used by the boatmen of the lake. Any Sunday these paddle-makers can be found in the market in the city of Pátzcuaro. (One man from Pichátaro also takes wooden chairs to the Pátzcuaro market.)

In the matter of woodworking the Tarascans were noted at the time of the Conquest. It amounted almost to a cult at that time and has remained a strong part of their culture pattern. In a document of 1788 it was noted as being the only outstanding craft endeavor in Pichátaro.[39] Today it is the most important and most spectacular of the skills. There are nearly a dozen men in Pichátaro now known to the villagers as "maestros" in woodworking, fine craftsmen working with an aesthetic sense. They are not mere repairmen as is the case with the carpenters in Hispanic towns.

Most of the houses of Pichátaro, as in many towns of the mountain Tarascans, are built of sawed logs. Formerly these logs were hewn. The carving of the pillars, capitals, lintels, and door frames

Hand hewn log cabin, Pichátaro

as well as other parts of the house is done with the fine precision of a craftsman.[40] The lich gate with its two-slope roof may have been introduced into this woodworking country by churchmen or it may have been developed with some idea of utility. Indians now

[39]AGN, *Ramo de História*, Vol. 73, Expediente 18, p. 101.
[40]The quality of the carving is declining, however.

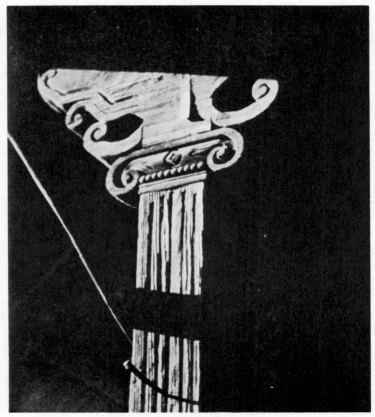

Detail of carving. House in Pichátaro

justify them by saying that they protect the gate against the rain. In view of their elaboration and the comparative simplicity of the gates this is hardly reasonable. It seems to be just another opportunity to exercise their skill in carving and to satisfy their aesthetic desires and love of the craft. Woodworkers also occupy themselves in making chairs, tables, and other household furniture.

There are many good weavers. Some of the handsomest of the native woolen blankets are made by the men of Pichátaro. Women weave belts in both men's and women's types and napkins of cotton. There is one weaver of women's shawls.[41]

[41]Her craft is a new acquisition to the town. Her husband paid for her lessons in another village. It fits into the pattern of present Pichátaro. They are willing and anxious to add other crafts when they are useful.

Sweaters are "knitted" (with a buttonhook) on a wooden frame with a row of nails on either side of the elongated middle opening.

There are several hatmakers who weave the strips of palm fibre, purchased in the market at Erongarícuaro, and stitch them together on a sewing machine. At the end of the nineteenth century Pichátaro was the center for the manufacture of hats. Early in this century many of the hatmakers moved, due to chaotic political conditions, to a place of refuge on the island of Xarácuaro in Lake Pátzcuaro. The hat industry of Xarácuaro has become dominant in the area and only a remnant is left in Pichátaro. A few brooms are made from the palm fibre left over from the hatmaking process.

There are numerous masons, a craft obviously from Spain. The masons of Pichátaro may hire out by the day if they feel so inclined, but a proletarian class of masons has not been formed. With stone carving, as with wood, much of the effort expended cannot be explained in terms of cash value. Many of the streets are lined with walls of chiseled stone. The foundations of many of the log houses are made of shaped stone. In this there is clearly a pride of craftsmanship that is beyond mere utility.

Leatherworking is weakly represented in Pichátaro. There are enough shoemakers to supply the needs of the village but that is all. There is no attempt to make anything else nor to elaborate on their shoemaking process as they have with their Indian craft of woodworking. Tarascans, of course, worked leather and made a sort of shoe before the advent of the Spanish. There are no tanners in town. Presumably this activity has been appropriated by Hispanic towns and was never a strong enough part of the Tarascan village to be maintained.

There are no metal workers in Pichátaro.

Pátzcuaro

One of the larger valleys in the Volcanic Mountains is mostly filled by shallow Lake Pátzcuaro. On its sloping shores and on its islands are a score of villages, many of which have a long-pre-Conquest history. It was one of the areas of concentrated Tarascan settlement.

The alluvium of the lake shore and the slopes of the surrounding hills were the basis of a productive native agriculture. Fishing is an ancient and important activity. Transport by dug-out canoes has tied these lake villages together from long before the time that the first Europeans saw them to the present. Spaniards quickly recognized the quality and attractions of the region and established themselves in personal control of the choice bits of land.

On the gently sloping land at the south end of the lake, at about two miles from the shore, the city of Pátzcuaro is located. It is a site that was used by the Tarascans for one of their settlements. At one time it had been a settlement of importance, but by the time of the Conquest it had lost most of its population and consisted of less than a dozen huts.

Its importance was again established when a Spanish bishop decided to transfer the cathedral and seat of provincial government to Pátzcuaro in 1538. By Spanish decree this settlement of less than a dozen families became, within a few months, the chief city of the province of Michoacán, and an important Spanish administrative center. The large number of Spaniards who moved into the settlement so greatly over-shadowed the few Indians that they were effectively lost in an Hispanic city. However, it remained an important center of exchange for the surrounding Indian territory by reason of its cross-roads position.[42]

Although it lost its political and ecclesiastical pre-eminence before the end of that first century, it has remained a center of affairs for the inhabitants of the general area, white, Indian, and the mixtures thereof. That it retained this function is in no way due to the qualities of the inhabitants of the city who, by the end of the sixteenth century had settled back in complacent and pious comfort. Pátzcuaro has remained locally important because of its distinct positional advantages. It served and serves as the center for the many routes that converge upon it from the lake and mountain villages. The Indians have made its plaza their market headquarters.

Around the plazas are the homes built for the Spanish families, many of them direct descendants of the Conquistadores, who lived in somnolent satisfaction.

We have an official report for the year 1788. At that time the census included 1,837 Spanish, 1,113 mulattos, and 389 mestizos— no Indians.[43] It was a quiet conservative city whose lovely plazas were encircled by the homes of the aristocratic landowning fami-

[42]Dan Stanislawski, "The Political Rivalry of Pátzcuaro and Morelia, an Item in the Sixteenth Century Geography of Mexico," in *Annals of the Association of American Geographers*, Vol. XXXVII, September, 1947, No. 3, pp. 135–144.

[43]AGN, *Ramo de História*, Vol. 73, Expediente 18, p. 3.

Colonial homes on the main plaza. Pátzcuaro

lies with incomes not only from the lands in the immediate basin but from sugar estates on the warm slope to the south and from copper mines in Inguarán and San Chiqueo.

The chaos of early nineteenth century political changes had little permanent effect upon Pátzcuaro, for only two generations ago Lumholz found it to be a "dull place with lots of priests and masses." Even the railroad that was completed in 1886 had little effect upon the city. It was then what it had become at the end of the sixteenth century—a charming little city dominated by clerics, administrators, and leisure class aristocrats.

The twentieth century has seen much of this changed. The landholding families have been stripped of their properties; the priests no longer hold the same official places in society. Perhaps the most revolutionary change of all is taking place now. Due to the completion of the highway, Pátzcuaro is now in the process of transformation into a tourist center. Pátzcuaro has lived through centuries of time and shown little inclination toward radical change. Her colonial quality may survive even in spite of tourists.

Pátzcuaro differs from the other settlements studied not only in the attitude of the early settlers and their descendants but also by reason of its greater importance and size. There probably has been a greater emphasis upon "services" even from colonial times for it had a distinct leisure class. An emphasis upon "services" continues, for now the demand comes from tourists. There are more doctors here proportionately than in the other towns. There are several hotels. It has a museum, a library, a garage, a telephone and telegraph office, a sewing machine agency, and street cars (horse-drawn). It has four establishments that could be classed as factories as several workmen are employed. Due to these special characteristics of Pátzcuaro, the usefulness of the crude count of individual locations and their activities is diminished. However, it is not far along the route of industrialization, and the method of "anatomical dissection" still serves. In spite of revolutions, creole and proletarian, in spite of tourism, in spite of certain "factory" production, Pátzcuaro exhibits in its anatomy clear and important traces of its background, and its present quality can be better understood in terms of this background.

Perhaps the first thing one notices about the map is the pattern of streets. The grid was established in Mexico before the settlement of Pátzcuaro. As the town was being established upon virtually unoccupied land, the grid was possible, and there was a conscious attempt to use it. However, as a document of 1581 recognized, "it is seated upon uneven ground and the streets are not as well ordered as in the other pueblos established nearby."[44]

Secondly, there are far more plazas and churches than in any other of the towns studied. One of its churches was built to be the Cathedral of Michoacán. It was originally designed to be the seat of the bishop and the center of ecclesiastical affairs. It maintained a greater degree of enthusiasm for the church, presumably because of its conservative landholding gentry. It retained more of the attitude of feudal Spain.

There is a disproportionately large number of fine houses in Pátzcuaro. The only other town comparable in this respect is Tacámbaro. There, on a smaller scale, one finds the same thing, and it is due, apparently, to the conservative landholding families that dominated Tacámbaro through most of its history.

---

[44]*Relación de la ciudad de Pátzcuaro* by Bachiller Juan Martínez, 8 de abril de 1581, reprinted in Manuel Toussaint, *Pátzcuaro*, 231–235.

In comparing Pátzcuaro, in this regard, with Ário and Purépero, which are somewhat comparable in size, the difference is striking. Such fine homes do not exist in either of the latter two. Neither Ário nor Purépero was the home city of aristocratic owners of great estates. Both of them were founded upon and developed by commerce.

Some commerce has always been a part of the life of Pátzcuaro by reason of her excellent position. Although her aristocracy neglected the full commercial possibilities, positions of advantage and probably of honor were allowed to the *mesones*, the places of shelter for mule-drivers and their animals. According to our tastes and views with regard to city planning, a shelter for transport workers is not held in high esteem and would not be found ordinarily in or near the best residential district. The Spanish attitude, in the towns of this inquiry at least, was otherwise. The *meson* is in a position of respect in all places, and this is particularly notable in Pátzcuaro, the most Spanish town of them all.

There are now thirteen *mesones* in Pátzcuaro. It seems that *mesones* are conservative institutions, for a map of the city made over a half century ago shows that the most important of the present *mesones* were then in the same locations. There is no available information as to the number or position of them in earlier periods, but it seems fair to assume that they have always been in the same or similar locations.

An interesting point with regard to *mesones* is their position relative to the churches. In virtually all cases in Pátzcuaro, the important *mesones* are in front of or next to churches. This is a position of high honor, in a Catholic country, and in view of the fact that the instruction from the Spanish monarch in the sixteenth century insisted that the church be located "in a position of honor" in the settlement.[45]

The basic crafts accompanying mule-driving are here. Leather-working, almost a monopoly of Spaniards or mestizos, is in the

---

[45]In Pátzcuaro most of the *mesones* are named for the churches nearby, e.g., "del Salvador," "San Antonio," "San Francisco," "San Juan de Dios," "San Agustín," "del Socorro," "San Cristóbal."

The study of the anatomy of the various settlements has convinced me that there must be a new appraisal of the views and attitudes of colonial Spaniards. The common view has assumed that the Spaniards were all trying to be aristocrats or priests and that mundane matters were despised. It seems from my evidence that this is not so. There apparently was a class of traders, highly respected, conservative and inarticulate who maintained the exchange of commodities necessary to the country. They were given recognition tacitly and although not highly rewarded, held a distinct place in society. It may be that the transfer of goods by pack animals was so necessary, immemorially old and respected that it was unremarked.

best position. The shoemakers are the only craftsmen on the plaza. All of them are near it or on the position of second importance on one of the main arterials. The tanneries are in the position originally assigned to them in the sixteenth century by the Spanish king, on the stream outside of town.[46]

---

[46]The royal instructions said to place them downstream from town so that the water used in the settlement would not be polluted. When they were established, they undoubtedly fulfilled these requirements, but now the town has grown out to them and some of the dwellings are downstream.

The number of metalworkers—tin, iron, and silver—in Pátzcuaro is fitting to its size in comparison with the other dominantly
Hispanic settlements. Their position is somewhat superior to the
Indian crafts of woolworking but certainly inferior to that of the
leatherworkers. Tourist trade of the last ten years has brought
two or three metalworkers into positions near the plaza. This is
not where one would expect to find them based upon evidence from
other settlements. The metalworker seemingly was not an honored
person in the colonial society of Michoacán.

There are few "Indian" crafts in Pátzcuaro. Such as do exist
are in the worst positions. With minor exceptions they are found
at the extreme edge of the city and away from the arterials.
Weaving is the occupation in only six locations. There are also
several single examples of "Indian" crafts.

In the last three or four years some of the "Indian" crafts have
become popular with the tourist trade and have been appropriated
by mestizos. These move into superior locations. For example,
there are now shops exhibiting painted or lacquered wooden bowls
on the plaza. The owners are mestizos.

Woodworking in general is weakly represented in Pátzcuaro,
but unlike Indian pueblos where it often is distinctly a creative
craft, here it is mostly a matter of repair carpentry. Perhaps it
should be more accurately listed under "services." Carpenters
are widely scattered in Pátzcuaro but are usually in inferior
positions and near the periphery. The map of the distribution of
all activities exhibits in typically Hispanic fashion the greatest concentration around the two main plazas. Again in typical manner
there are streamers of density out from the main routes of transport. The most important of these is clearly that to the lake. It
indicates one of Pátzcuaro's functions. This is the connection
between the old Hispanic city and the lake Indians. Few of the
Indians have ever lived in Pátzcuaro, but they certainly have put
their stamp upon its anatomy. The streamer of second importance
is that which bifurcates near the eastern edge of town, one road
being the old "camino real" to Morelia, the capital, the other divid-
ing again, with one of its prongs leading to a settlement of mountain Indians and the other to Tacámbaro and the hot country beyond it. There is still a suggestion of the former importance of
the Uruapan route in the southwest of the city. This remnant

Indians at the Pátzcuaro market

is all that is left of what must have been an important mule trail over a half century ago when there was no railroad from Uruapan.

The association of the best place for commerce and the preferred location for living is obvious. The large plaza of Pátzcuaro that is crowded with Indians on its two market days each week is the site of the former home of the Counts of Villa Hermosa de Alfaro and other colonial "families of quality." And as the second best location for trade is along the ganglia of trade, so is the second best location for houses.

Shopkeeping, in terms of the anatomy, was anything but degrading.

Erongarícuaro

Erongarícuaro is situated on the flat surface of a bluff at the western side of Lake Pátzcuaro. At the time of the Spanish assumption of authority over Michoacán, it was an administrative subdivision of the Tarascan capital, Tzintzuntzan. It was a village of trading importance at that time because it is the lake shore terminus for one of the more important mountain routes. The position makes a settlement here almost inevitable. Long before the Spaniards came, it was an Indian market center where lake

Erongarícuaro

Tarascans met their Tarascan mountain relatives for the exchange of goods.

The Spaniards were conscious of trade and the advantages of trading position. This place of exchange between lake and mountain Tarascans offered a profitable opportunity for Iberian middlemen. Spanish merchants and landholders established themselves. It was made a *cabecera*, an administrative center, with authority over the nearby lake pueblos as well as some of those on the mountain slope behind.[47]

Its importance was always limited, however, It has never been more than a secondary center of trade and administration since the time of the Conquest because Pátzcuaro, the larger city, is close-by and has always eclipsed it. Largely for this reason, it has never become fully Hispanicized and has retained Indian qualities lacking in Pátzcuaro.

The Spaniards "settled" Erongarícuaro in the regular grid pattern. Presumably this was done in the 1530's, at the time Pátzcuaro was "settled." According to royal instructions for waterside locations, the church in Erongarícuaro was placed eccentric to the town, on the highest point of land overlooking the water. It was given the place of honor required by the "Catholic Kings."

[47]Luis García Pimentel, *op. cit.*, 33.

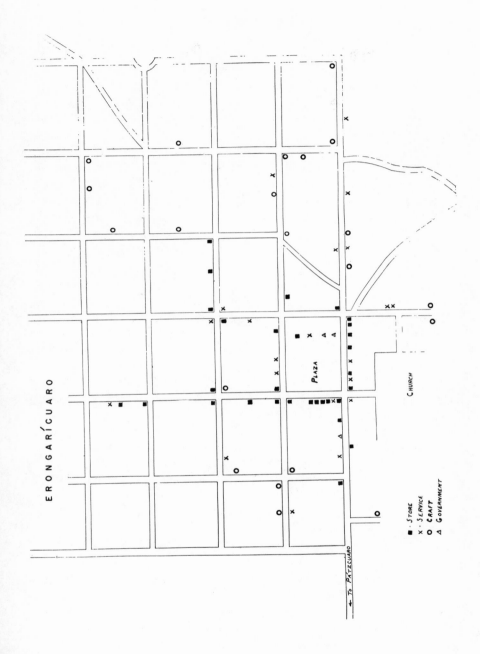

ERONGARÍCUARO

PLAZA

CHURCH

← To Pátzcuaro

■ Store
x Service
○ Craft
△ Government

One's first impression of Erongarícuaro is that of an "Hispanic" commercial town. Its streets are straight, clean, and, for the most part, neatly cobbled. Only by inquiry into its anatomy do the surviving Indian traits come to light. Then it appears that

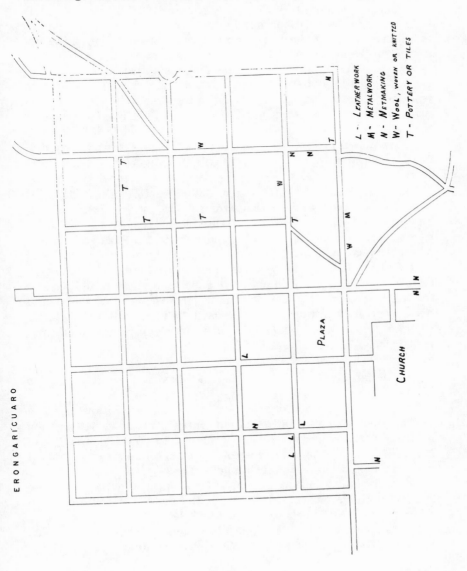

Erongarícuaro is a "dual-character" town. Spanish and Indian traits have associated here for over four centuries without forming a new compromise character.

In studying the map, the first point to be noted is the scattered distribution of activities. This suggests an Indian quality. It is suggestive of the distribution in the Indian village of Pichátaro more than it is of the pronounced plaza concentration to be observed in Hispanic settlements. But on closer observation this must be qualified, for there is some emphasis upon the plaza position. The leading storekeeper is located upon it. He is a mestizo who moved into town from outside of the area. His store and his way of business might fit into any of the fully Hispanic towns of the state. His house, behind his store, is one of the best in town.

In fashion typical of the Hispanic settlement (that is, typical insofar as the evidence adduced in this investigation is concerned) the *meson* has a place of honor, near the plaza and near the church.

Crafts, such as exist in this essentially commercial town, include both Indian and Iberian occupations. The native craft of net-making is associated with an inferior place. It happens, however, that it is found mainly on the slope next to the lake so it is not possible to say whether it was pushed there by reason of its being an inferior position relative to the plaza, or whether it was chosen as one of superior convenience for fishermen. One would assume the latter except for the fact that this convenience of position is not a very good argument with regard to Tarascans. The matter of time involved in going from home to work is not important. Indian society is not a wage society, and evaluation of time in terms of money is a concept strange to it.

The Indian craft of weaving does not have a favorable position in town.

Tile and pottery making are at the outskirts. Pottery making can be either a mestizo or an Indian craft in this area. Its position in Erongarícuaro suggests that it is Indian. Tile making is an Hispanic craft. It is not, however, a cottage industry but one of the open field. It is normally found at the edge of settlement.

There is an extension of importance from the plaza toward the north on the street that leads to the mountain route and another on the street to the southwest that leads to Pátzcuaro.

Erongarícuaro, like Chilchota, has some of both Indian and Hispanic traits and attitudes. Neither is dominant.

Its function is that of an intermediary between mountain and lake and, since the Conquest, between Indian and Hispanic producers. On market day the Indians of the mountains bring pine wood which is bartered for fish (although it is a matter of barter, the exchange is decided in terms of "reales," a colonial Spanish coin). Mountain Indians bring their surplus maize which they sell for cash. Palm fronds are brought in from the warm southern

Erongarícuaro market

slopes toward the Balsas River. Mountain Indians tear them into strips and braid them. Some of these braids they make into hats. Those that are not so used are brought to the Erongarícuaro market to sell to the hatmakers from the islands of Xarácuaro (who may have sold them the palm fronds originally). Buyers from beyond the boundaries of the state come to purchase pottery.

Chilchota

Chilchota lies at the lower end of a fertile mountain valley at about 5,800 feet elevation. Probably the site was not used prior

Outside of Chilchota

Threshing at outskirts of Chilchota

to the Conquest but was soon chosen by the Spaniards to be a place of settlement. The reasons are not hard to find. The fertile soils, the flat surface for plow agriculture, water in abundance from nearby springs, good climate (Cwa) all were obvious. More than this, there was Indian labor in the hills adjacent. The Indian settlements of the slopes were moved by Spanish order onto the lowland, and before the end of the sixteenth century most, if not all, of the present ten settlements in the valley were established.[48]

Adding greater importance to the settlement was the establishment of the main route from Mexico City to the west of Mexico which led through the valley and Chilchota. At the outset it was chosen as the local administrative center. Spaniards took up land nearby. Spanish and mestizo mule-drivers made it a way station. All of this made it more Hispanicized than the other towns of the valley.

In the first generation of Spanish control the inhabitants of the valley were forced by tribute requirements to raise wheat, a grain of European provenience.[49] This was continued over a long enough time to make it an integral part of the agricultural complex. Still La Cañada, as the valley is called, devotes itself to the European grain to a far greater extent than is normal to most parts of the area.[50] The cotton weavers of the general area quickly recognized the value of the European sheep and substituted wool for cotton in the weaving industry.

During the colonial period the percentage of mestizos increased with a corresponding decrease in the percentage of Indians. By 1750 more than half of the population was mestizo.[51] Now it is considered to be a mestizo town.[52] This is certainly the first impression that one might get, but it is misleading. The Tarascan language has disappeared "except for a few old folks," but Indian ways and attitudes have not entirely been forgotten. Some are

[48]Biblioteca Nacional, Madrid, Real Academia de la Historia, *Ynformación hecha por un ynstrucción de el pueblo de Chilchota*, 1579, Oct. 15 (12-18-3), num. 16, VI, 22 ff., including 2 ff. of quest. printed instructions, cited in Jiménez LCXXVII, p. 10.

[49]West, *op. cit.*, 48.

[50]Several Indian recipes have been altered in La Cañada to use wheat instead of corn.

[51]West, *op. cit.*, map no. 8.

[52]West, *op. cit.*, map no. 11.

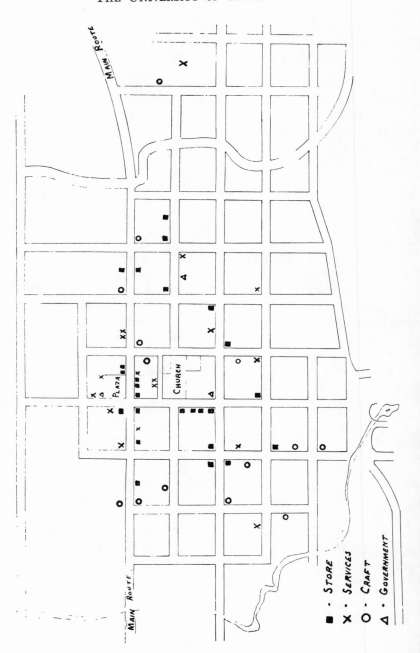

continued intact, and others have become part of a new "dual-character." This is indicated by its anatomy.[53]

The plaza and the through route of colonial times show a slight superiority in density and quality, but it is far from the dominance to be observed in purely Hispanic settlements. The activities are fairly well scattered.

The quality of houses is somewhat higher near the plaza. For example, the only houses with windows are either near the plaza or on the through route. But there is no sharp difference from the houses at the periphery. Nor do people in town feel that there is much to be desired in living near the plaza.

The church is a block from the plaza. Whether this indicates that the Hispanic influence was less than in other towns cannot be said. It is true that in all of La Cañada, the church has a less dominant position than is the average for Mexico.

The distribution and number of crafts indicates a "dual-character." There are some Indian crafts—for example, there are three blanket weavers. Judged by relation to the plaza, they are in inferior positions.

The Spanish leather crafts are represented by one tannery, as well as by shoemaking and miscellaneous leather workers. As one would expect, their position reflects their Hispanic background. They are all on or near the main route. In numbers and importance they cannot be compared in proportion to population with those of the fully Hispanic settlements such as Pátzcuaro, Purépero, Ário, and Tacámbaro. The tannery is offside but this was because of the location of the stream.

The importance of transport and the mule-driver is shown by the four *corrales,* all in good locations (two near the church, two abutting upon the plaza).

Chilchota still serves as the commercial center for the western two-thirds of the valley. Although mule-driving is losing out to the truck, it hasn't been completely submerged as is shown by the existence of the four *corrales.* The wheat, introduced by the Spanish 400 years ago, is still being grown but now to be sold for cash and not to be paid in tribute. The more rapid transport of

---

[53]It has been assumed by some anthropologists that the absence of the native tongue indicates the "mestizization" of a town. In the study of anatomy it seems that the idea of "mestizization" is not serviceable. In both Chilchota and Erongarícuaro one does not hear the native tongue spoken, but in each town there are important Indian survivals.

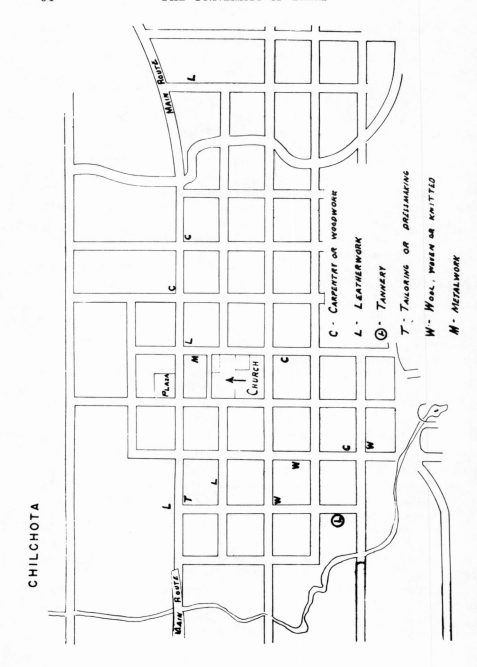

the present has made another change profitable. Now Indians and mestizos have entered into the business of truck farming.

Purépero

Purépero was established at the northern edge of the Tarascan mountain region of Michoacán. It is not quite far enough north nor quite low enough in elevation to be included as a part of the Bajío. Its site is a large, gently sloping, relatively level plain circumscribed by low hills. It is somewhat more arid than its neighboring settlements. It falls within the Cwb area.

Among Mexican towns Purépero is a comparative newcomer. In the general report of settlements in the Spanish colonies which was made during the last generation of the eighteenth century, it was not mentioned.[54] As all of the other settlements of the region were described in this report and in church lists, it seems clear that Purépero did not exist at that time. However, it must have been founded shortly thereafter, for by 1822 it had become a place of size and importance.[55] It continued to grow and by the middle of the nineteenth century was noted for its farflung lines of trade.

Town records are almost non-existent, but informants whose families had lived in the town for several generations spoke confidently of the foundation having taken place "over a century ago" on lands given for the purpose by a Spanish landowner. They also agreed that the reason for settlement was to protect mule-trains from the depredations of bandits who lurked in the hills nearby. All agree that a stopping place for the pack-trains was convenient at about this location.

During the last quarter of the eighteenth century the Spanish government greatly reduced its restrictions on trade within the colonies. This made trade possible in regions where it had been lacking or weak previously. Also, in the general weakening of Spanish control, banditry probably became more profitable. It would not be surprising if both of these factors were important in the establishment and growth of Purépero.

This relatively dry country may never have been used for agriculture until settled by these mule-drivers. They are positive in their statements that there never were haciendas here. A farm of a little over 200 acres is the largest known, and this is exceptional.

[54] AGN, *Ramo de História*, Vol. 73, Expediente 18.
[55] Martínez de Lejarza, *op. cit.*, 236.

The mule-driver apparently took only enough land for the use of his family. His interest was mule transport and not landholding.

In addition to raising the basic necessities such as wheat, maize, and beans, the men of Purépero have pastured herds of cattle on the hills, and one sees many herds of goats. It is not known whether the goats are responsible for the deterioration of the lands or if they were introduced when the lands would support no other animal. The local inhabitants have no answer to the question which may mean that the goat was introduced early.

These men of Purépero, far less interested in agriculture than in commerce, have scarred what may have been a more promising landscape. Probably due to its climate, this little area was one of greater hazard than those of the Tarascan mountain valleys and slopes to the south and the Bajío lands to the north. The lands are deteriorating. There is deep gullying just outside the settlement.

In the memory of many inhabitants the hills near-by were covered with stands of pines. They say that "it used to be easier to get wood." If it was ever "easy to get wood," things have changed, for the hills surrounding the settlement are now bare.

In the early days—but within the memory of present inhabitants—water was plentiful. Much of it came from springs along the foot of a nearby slope. This, informants say, was blocked from use by the town by "a Spaniard." Whether there was a change in the control of the source of water at the time of the early twentieth century revolutions or not could not be determined. Now the town is suffering from a shortage of water. In view of the stripping of the nearby hills and the gullying on all of the nearby slopes, it seems hardly necessary to introduce "a Spaniard" as the villain of the piece. Wells have been dug in almost all of the lots in town but, by reports, as time goes on the old wells no longer serve and the new ones must be deepened. At the low east end of town the owners of wells pump water into jugs and water wagons and drive either hurros laden with large jugs or water wagons through town each day selling water.

Undoubtedly this town was settled by mule-drivers. It grew, it seems, by the increase of its original families. There are no "foreigners" in town nor does any inhabitant remember an intrusive family.

PURÉPERO

■ - STORE
✗ - SERVICE
○ - CRAFT
△ - GOVERNMENT
● - FACTORY

N

Many of the traits of the inhabitants suggest a fairly pure Iberian background. It is notable that the skin color is distinctly lighter than that seen in most Mexican mestizo settlements. There are many light eyes and some almost blonde hair.

During the summer of each year a fiesta is organized by the bakers. The townsfolk state categorically that it is an old Spanish baker's fiesta. In it one of the characters represents the coal for the baker's oven. This could hardly have been Mexican. It suggests an importation from Asturias.

Prior to this last generation Purépero mule-drivers went into and across the hot Lowland of the Balsas and south through Mexico, even into Guatemala. From the great cattle haciendas of the Lowland they picked up hides, cheese, leather goods, cascalote for tanning, and a miscellany of other products. Most of these were delivered on the central plateau of Mexico. Some may have been carried into Guatemala to be exchanged for cacao and other items for the return trip. For a century Purépero was a center for mule traffic.

Now there is a new highway which connects most of the important settlements. The trucks have spelled out the doom of the mule trains of Purépero. The decline began about a generation ago, but it was not felt sharply at that time. Many of the mule-drivers, who were men accustomed to movement and to strange places, went to California to work in the steel plants of Torrance or Pittsburgh. This ended with the end of the lush "twenties" but the savings that they had laid away postponed their real depression. In the "thirties" the pinch began to be felt. By 1940 the population had fallen to a little over 7,000 from the 1921 figure of 9,000. The decline continues.

The pattern of streets suggests that at the beginning there was an attempt to establish a grid. The plaza is approximately rectangular, and streets leave it at right angles or nearly so. However, they do not continue far before they strike off at strange angles or contort themselves to flout the king's regulations. It seems very likely that the opinion of several informants is correct that the streets took shape from the route chosen by the mule trains. This can be believed easily from the pattern. This was a wooded area, and the pack mules could not strike a straight course. They did have to choose places to cross the stream canyons which we may suppose had more water in them at the time of set-

Purépero

tlement than they have at present. The streets crossing these ravines always bend to meet them at right angles.

The best houses of town are on or near the plaza. A lot here is worth about four times as much as one of the same size on the outskirts. This seems to be a matter of tradition more than of commercial advantage, for the plaza in Purépero is neither active nor impressive. There is very little retail trade. The most prosperous stores are those selling drygoods. This is not surprising in an Hispanic town. (It is even more striking in Arteaga.) The most numerous stores are the meat markets. This points to a special quality in Purépero. The number of meat markets is smaller in other Hispanic settlements. This may mean a high average prosperity, or perhaps it indicates a special group of settlers with special dietary attitudes. On Sundays it has more activity due to the fact that the Indians from one end of the Cañada assemble here for their market. Also milk and cheese venders from Tlazazalca, mestizo-soap plant venders, and a scattering of miscellaneous peddlers add to the Sunday activity. Sun-

day, however, is only a brief interlude in the week. Purépero clearly is not a place cf retail activity. Its business has been transport.

The finest homes belong to store owners, but in all cases these store owners were also owners of mule trains. Their homes are not comparable to those of aristocratic Pátzcuaro. They are middle-class homes. In the fashion typical of Hispanic settlements the quality of homes decreases in terms of distance from the plaza, except for those on the streets of traffic.

The roofs of all houses are of tile, even including the inferior homes on the outskirts. The shingles of Indian villages are unthinkable it would seem. The eaves are extraordinarily long. In this respect only Ário de Rosales is comparable. The carpenters of town are largely occupied in the carving of the long eave timbers.

The single church is not impressive considering the size of the town. Compared to Pátzcuaro, which is roughly comparable in size, this points to somewhat casual interest in religion in Purépero. The position of the church also suggests a casual attitude. It is not on the high point of town. This may result from the late settlement of Purépero, settlement after the time of strict obedience to the royal instructions, or it may have been a choice between the high point of town, at the outskirts, and the plaza in the center. But, in any event, the opinion expressed in the office of the *Presidencia* seems to be valid, that "they were mostly Catholic but not fanatical."

Frequently men go into the business of processing the things that they transport. The men of Purépero went into the leather business. Whether or not they had their own herds of cattle in the beginning does not matter. For as long as any of them can remember leatherworking has been important. They bring both hides and cascalote pods from the hot country. Much of the cascalote is handled commercially into the shoe center at León, to the north, but much of it remains in Purépero to tan the leather that is there made into shoes, huaraches, and miscellaneous leather goods. They also tan leather for sale to shoemakers of other towns.

The settlement probably never had a rich man. On the other hand, from present evidence there probably was little if any poverty. These are industrious middle-class people and presumably always have been. There are no loiterers in the plaza. Like other mule-skinners of Michoacán they are hard working and sober. There is no alcoholic liquor made in Purépero. Saloons are unimportant.

The anatomy map clearly indicates streamers of activity. One runs north from the plaza and one to the northeast. These two converge in the route to La Piedad, an important Hispanic settlement of the Bajío. On the east and southeast are two extensions of activity. These two streets lead to the Cañada route. This serves not only the ten Indian villages but leads on to Zamora, an important Hispanic city.

The concentration of activities to the west of the plaza may be due to this being the side toward Tlazazalca, an early and formerly important settlement. The concentration on this side is mostly in terms of services. Retail stores are found in greater numbers on the other side of the plaza. The great gaps of inactivity between the commercial ganglia are notable, particularly to the east of the plaza.

Crafts are distinctly concentrated on the north and east of the plaza, mostly on the main routes. There seems to be no particular approbium connected with crafts except in the case of the weavers. Weaving is found at the extreme edge and is not associated with the main routes. The number of weavers is small. The product probably is sold to the Indians of La Cañada. Although the weavers are not Indians, this Indian craft seems to taint by association even a lighter skinned person.

Shoemakers are clearly the elite among craftsmen. They are the most numerous and widespread craftsmen in town. They are located almost entirely near the plaza or upon the streets of traffic.

Another concentration is that of the *mesones* and *corrales* for the mules and their drivers. All, with two exceptions, are to be found on the west or south and are well separated from the craft blocks. They are close to the plaza, with three facing upon it.[56] No one of them, however, is near the church.

The position of the tanneries is abnormal. This probably indicates the lateness of settlement. According to the early royal instructions it would have been impossible to place them as they are found in Purépero, many on the upstream side of town (the east).

---

[56]One of these latter claims to be a hotel but judging from the sign in the "lobby"—"It is prohibited to urinate on the floor"—it probably is more fittingly included with the *mesones*.

Carpenters are few in number and, although not on the plaza, are located on the main routes of traffic. This may be due to the demand in Purépero for carved eaves. The same seems true in Ário de Rosales where they are associated largely, in terms of position, with leatherworkers.

General Conclusions

1. Great persistence of culture groups.
2. The character of towns is largely based in the cultural background of the dominant group and this cannot be recognized casually. Probing into the anatomy of towns brings to light important survivals that will not otherwise be suspected.
3. The original function and purpose of a firmly established town tends to continue. For example, Ário de Rosales was a commercial town from its inception. It is now, in spite of changes in the economy and economic geography of Mexico, in spite of changes in transport, a commercial town. There is no question that its geographical position was excellent for precisely this function but there are other locations that might have assumed its function. They did not because Ário had supplied the service. Tacámbaro and Pátzcuaro continue, in spite of major changes in Mexico, to function much in the way that they have done. The same can be said of most of the other towns.
4. The presence or absence of certain traits in a town may be a clue to its period of settlement and its type of settlers. And this may be reversible, for granting the serviceability of the conclusions, if the type of settler and the time of settlement is known, one may have a fair indication of the character of the settlement, although obviously, the variations within the town and, indeed the activities, are altered by physical conditions.

The Qualities of the Hispanic Town

A. Historical-Cultural Aspects
 1. Prestige of the plaza and arterials
   This is true for homes as well as for all activities. Usually it includes all sides of the blocks contiguous to the plaza. The land is of higher price here and values diminish in all directions out from them with the exception of the properties along the arterials. Positional importance decreases less rapidly from the plaza toward the peripheries along these streets leading to the main cross-country routes.
 2. Social position of trade
   The retail merchants have, in general, choice positions. Invariably many of the best locations on the plaza are theirs. Most of the street corners along the arterials are occupied by retail stores.
   These are middlemen, and there is seldom any manufacturing connected with their activities. There was and is a New World middle class, Spanish or mestizo, not Indian. It has never been large but always, presumably, vitally important. Judging by their geographical position in towns, the individuals have long enjoyed prestige and respect.

In Pátzcuaro one of the merchants on the corner of the main plaza is considered to represent the finest graces of the disappearing colonial nobility. His family has been involved in trade through all known generations.

Usually the merchant lives with his store. There is no detachment of living from business. There is no desire to finish the disagreeable work of the day so that one can remove himself to his home for his hours of enjoyment.

3. Economic prestige of mule-driving

The positions of the *mesones* is almost always favorable. This is surprising to one of the Anglo-American points of view. The stopping places of mules and their drivers are breeders of odors, flies, and presumably disease. In the sixteenth century the Spanish king issued explicit instructions to the effect that noisome and objectionable activities should be relegated to beyond the limits on the low side of town. This obviously wise regulation is still largely honored. But in the minds of Spaniards there could have been no idea that there was anything distressing about the *meson*. It has a location side by side with that of the most prosperous merchant or the grandest "grandee" of town. They are intimately associated with the plazas or are among the better locations of the chief arterials.

There is, in most towns, a clear positional relation between the *meson* and the church—note especially Pátzcuaro, one of the oldest and certainly the most aristocratic of the towns. It points certainly to one conclusion, that mule-driving was an ancient and honored profession. Whether it was equally so in Iberia would be interesting to know. But why is it associated with the church? Did churchmen desire the association? Did they perhaps use mule-drivers in furthering their work? Or was it, a more probable explanation, a simple relation between two honored institutions of Hispanic life?

The *mesones* seem to have been among the most stable things in Páatzcuaro. Of those recorded in this study most appear on the map of 1895. It is entirely reasonable to assume that prior to 1895 they had been there for long generations.

4. Prestige of leather-working

The anatomy maps show that towns that are clearly Hispanic in background have a variety of craftsmen working in leather, making huaraches, shoes, gloves, vaqueros necessities, bridles and saddles. Their position in town is good. They do not have the preferred position of the storekeeper, but they are usually close to the plaza or on the arterials.

This again raises the question as to the type of persons who followed the professions. In Spain shoemaking and tanning were officially designated as "oficios viles y bajos."

Were there a group of depressed laborers in Spain who found new and better lives for themselves in the New World? Or did the necessities of the situation offer opportunities and prestige denied in Spain? In any event the record of this study seems clear beyond cavil.

5. The weakness of all crafts except leatherwork

Whatever other crafts exist are found located in inferior positions toward the periphery or in blind alley locations between the arterials. This is notably the case with regard to woolworking. Weavers are nearly always in the worst possible locations and never in the best. It is not true that Hispanic peoples and towns avoided textilemaking. In some of the towns considered in this paper cotton-weaving was important during colonial times and was in the hands of mestizos. It is probably true that they were never strongly interested in the weaving of wool. It seems that Indians at the cooler elevations were glad enough to relinquish cotton to the Hispanic peoples in exchange for wool.

Woodworking is absent or, if present, unimportant. This is probably a universal trait of Hispanic settlements. The lack of trees in such settlements probably reflects an age-old Iberian disinterest in trees and their products.

Metalworking is important nowhere.

Spain was a raw material producing country with income derived from her raw materials. The Moors had introduced crafts but presumably the Vizigoths after their reconquest looked with disfavor upon these crafts that had been in the hands of Moors and the Jews. The Spanish kings, at various times, had seen the advantage of craft development and had tried to promote them but with small success. If the evidence of town anatomy in Michoacán may be accepted, the basic Iberian attitude was transferred here.

6. Conservatism

After four centuries many of the traits shown in the anatomy of these towns are similar to those demanded in the sixteenth century. For example, the position of the slaughter houses, probably that of the *mesones* and the churches.

B. Distinction between Towns on the Basis of Function and Period of Settlement

1. Landholding (hacienda) towns
    e.g., Pátzcuaro, Tacámbaro
       Greatest prestige of plaza
       Best homes
       Services in greater number
2. Early commercial trade route towns
    e.g., Ário de Rosales and Tacámbaro
       Activities more evenly distributed
3. Mule-drivers towns
    e.g., Purépero, also Ário de Rosales and Tacámbaro
       Importance of leatherwork
       Importance of the arterials

In the above three groups there is one town in each group that stands out above the others as distinct in its class. For example, Pátzcuaro was the aristocratic seat of the great hacendados of the region. Tacámbaro was the town center for some haciendas but was clearly in second place to Pátzcuaro. Tacámbaro functioned also as a mule-drivers center. In its anatomy it shows the fine homes and their concentration on the plaza that would be expected from an hacienda center. It also shows the importance of the arterials and the distributional factors associated with mule traffic and trade routes. Ário has never been associated with the aristocracy. In times past there have been haciendas in greater importance than today. This may be reflected in its anatomy. But dominantly it is commercial. Purépero, designed almost completely by mule-drivers, shows this in the distribution along its arterials as well as in its leather crafts.

The Qualities of the Indian Town

1. Plaza unimportant
2. No positional value or prestige
3. Strength of Indian crafts
   Woodworking, weaving (although wool has supplanted the cotton of aboriginal Michoacán)
4. Weakness or absence of Hispanic activities
   No mule-driving. However, this may be true only of this area. In the colonial records there is evidence of Indian mule-drivers elsewhere. It seems that the Tarascans had little interest or that the particular Hispanic peoples of the area pre-empted the business.
   Almost no commerce in stores.
   Leatherwork of minor importance.
5. Town loosely constructed
   In the center of Pichátaro buildings are closer together than at the outskirts, which is probably the effect of the few mestizos who are concentrated on the main street. In fact, they undoubtedly have made it the "main street."
   The Indian towns of the Tarascan mountain region all suggest a transitional stage between the *rancheria* and the agglomerated town proper.
   The *solares* or town lots are large and serve as house gardens. The houses themselves may or may not face directly upon the street. There are large numbers of trees. In fact the towns often look more like wooded areas with houses scattered among trees than like towns with tres in them.[57]

The Dual-Character Town

There is not much to be said about the anatomy of the "dual-character" town except that it shows traits of both Hispanic and Indian towns.

It certainly lacks strong character. Mule-driving is usually present but weakly represented. No craft is strong although both Hispanic and Indian crafts may be found. In terms of the total number of activities the position is midway between the Hispanic and Indian towns.

---

[57]Compare maps of Pichátaro and Chilchota with those of the Hispanic towns of Apatzingán and Arteaga. They are roughly comparable in size.

The anatomy map in such a settlement probably shows the degree of dominance of either Indian or Hispanic character (not the number of people for the Spaniard will dominate with smaller numbers, especially in commerce).

Conclusions

In reviewing the work done and the results of it, one pronounced weakness is at once apparent. It is the need for more examples of Indian towns. One almost pure product and two with traits that are presumed to be Indian in the light of evidence from the one good example is hardly sufficient evidence. For a person who is acquainted with the area it seems tentatively acceptable, however, as there is no apparent discrepancy in terms of other Indian towns of the region even though they have not been dissected anatomically.

Obviously the ancient Indian craft of pottery making should not have been neglected. An inquiry should be made into the anatomy of a pottery-making village to compare it with Pichátaro. It is equally obvious that samples should be taken from other areas and other native culture groups as well as of Hispanic settlements in other environments.

This neglect was a product of an original assumption that anatomical differences would reflect regional difference. On the basis of that belief, the towns chosen for study had very little relation— only accidental—to racial and cultural groups.

That this assumption was erroneous was not apparent while the field work was being done or a different tack could have been taken. Unfortunately it did not come out clearly until all of the information had been mapped, studied, and reduced to generalizations. By this time the field had been left behind.

BIBLIOGRAPHY

UNPUBLISHED ARCHIVAL MATERIALS

Madrid, Biblioteca Nacional
  Relación of the Bishopric of Michoacán, 1620, Sept. 20.
    Original Bib. Palacio, Madrid in MS. 2579, 24 ff. (unnumbered), Catálogo No. 267, Vol. 11.
Real Academia de la Historia
  Ynformación hecha por un ynstrucción de el pueblo de Chilchota, 1579, Oct. 15 (12-18-3), num. 16, VI, 22 ff., including 2 ff. of quest. printed instructions, cited in Jiménez LCXXVII.
Mexico, Archivo General de la Nación (AGN)
  Ramo de História, Vol. 73, Expediente 18
Sevilla, Archivo General de Indias
  Minas de Metal descubierta en Michoacán, México, 1599 (Sevilla, Archivo General de Indias, Audiencia de México, leg. 258, 60–1–41. 40 ff.)
University of Texas, Latin-American Collection.
  Descripción de Tancítaro hecha de orden de su corregidor Sebastián Macarro, a 27 de Septiembre de 1580. Original. 11 fojas.

PUBLISHED MATERIALS

Basalenque, Diego. *Historia de la Provincia de San Nicolás de Tolentino de Michoacán, del Orden de N.P.S. Augustín* (Mexico: Tip. Barbedillo y Cía., 1886).

Contreras Arias, Alfonso. *Mapa de las provincias climatológicas de la República Mexicana*. Secretaría de Agricultura y Fomento, Mexico, 1942.

Gálvez, Vicente. *Hidrogeología de la Zona de Aguililla* (Mexico: Tip. La Impresora, 1937).

García Pimentel, Luis. *Relación de los Obispados de Tlaxcala, Michoacán, Oaxaca y otros lugares en el siglo XVI*. Manuscrito de la colección del Señor Don Joaquín García Icazbalceta, Mexico, 1904.

Memoria presentada por el cuidadano General de división Manuel González al ejecutivo de la unión (Morelia: Imprenta del Govierno, en palacio, 1877).

Kelly, Isabel. *Excavations at Apatzingán, Michoacán*, Viking Fund Publications in Anthropology, Number Seven, New York, 1947.

Martínez de Lejarza, Juan José. *Análisis estadístico de la Provincia de Michuacan* (Mexico: Imprenta Nacional del Supremo Gobierno de los Estados Unidos, en Palacio, 1824).

Paso y Troncoso, Francisco del. *Papeles de Nueva España. Segunda Serie, Geografía y estadística*. Vol. 1. Madrid, 1905.

Ponce, Fray Alonso. *Relación breve y verdadera de algunas cosas de las muchas que sucedieron al padre Fray Alonso Ponce en las provincias de la Nueva España. . . .* (Madrid: Imprenta de la Viuda de Calero, 1873).

Relación de las ceremonias y ritas y población y governación de los Indios de la provincia de Michuacan hecha al illmo. Señor Don Antonio de Mendoza virrey y governador de esta Nueva España por S.M. (?) G. Morelia. Tip. de A. Aragon, 1903. (commonly known as Relación de Michoacán).

Robles Ramos, Ing. Ramiro. "Orogenesis de la República Mexicana en Relación a su Relieve Actual," *Irrigación en México*, V. 23, No. 3, May-June, 1942.

Romero, José Guadalupe. *Noticias para formar la historia y la estadística del Obispado de Michoacán, Mexico.* (Imprenta de Vicente y García Torres, 1862.)

Romero Flores, Jesús. *Tacámbaro*, Mexico, 1939.

Standley, Paul C. *Trees and Shrubs of Mexico*, Contributions from the United States National Herbarium, Vol. 23, Washington, 1921–1926.

Stanislawski, Dan
    (a) "Early Spanish Town Planning in the New World," in *The Geographical Review*, Vol. XXXVII, No. 1, 1947, pp. 95–105.
    (b) "Tarascan Political Geography," in *American Anthropologist*, Vol. 49, No. 1, Jan.–March, 1947.
    (c) "The Political Rivalry of Pátzcuaro and Morelia, an Item in the Sixteenth Century Geography of Mexico," in *Annals of the Association of American Geographers*, Vol. XXXVII, September, 1947, No. 3, pp. 135–144.

Storm, Marian. *Hoofways into Hot Country* (Mexico, 1939).

Toussaint, Manuel. *Pátzcuaro* (Mexico: Imprenta Universitaria, 1942).

Velasco, Alfonso Luis. *Geografía y Estadística de la República Mexicana*, Tomo VI, Geografía y Estadística del Estado de Michoacán de Ocampo, May, 1890.

Villaseñor y Sánchez, D. Antonio de. *Parte que Corresponde a Michoacán en la estadística que con el nombre de TEATRO AMERICANO . . .*, (Morelia: Imprenta de Ignacio Arango, 1852).

West, Robert C. *Cultural Geography of the Modern Tarascan Area*, Smithsonian Institution, Institute of Social Anthropology Publication No. 7 (Washington, 1948).

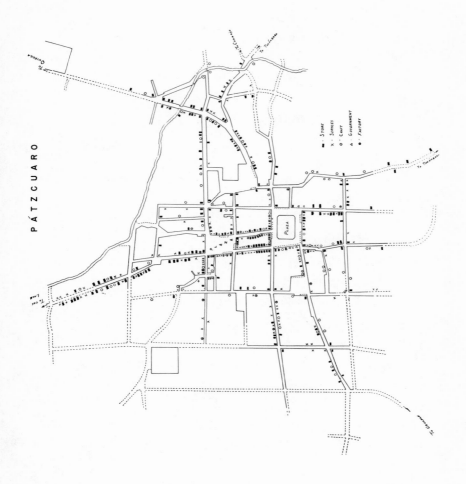

P Á T Z C U A R O